Keynote

Communication in the Real World

Michael Rost
Anne McGannon

LINGUAL HOUSE

Keynote

ISBN   textbook 0 582 10235 9   manual 0 582 10233 2   cassette set 0 582 10225 1

Copyright © 1993 Longman Group UK Ltd. All rights reserved. No part of this publication or related recordings and manuals may be reproduced, including by way of photocopying, stored in a retrieval system, or transmitted in any form or by any means without prior written permission from the publisher.

This book was developed for Longman Group by Lateral Communications, Ltd.

5   4   3   2   1

Printed in Hong Kong

text design: Hal Hershey
cover design: Kotaro Kato
project coordinator: Keiko Kimura
text illustrators: Ellen Sasaki, Marilyn Hill, Valerie Randall
photographs: Ken Kitamura, Keiko Kimura
recording supervisor: David Joslyn

Lingual House
A division of Longman ELT
Longman Group UK Ltd.
Longman House
Harlow
Essex CM20 2JE
ENGLAND

Longman Japan
1-13-19 Sekiguchi
Bunkyo-ku
Tokyo 112
JAPAN

Acknowledgements

The Publisher wishes to thank the following copyright holders for permission to adapt their material for use in this book:

Dorothee L. Mella. *The Language of Color*. New York: Warner Books, 1988.

E.D. Hirsch, Jr. *A First Dictionary of Cultural Literacy*. Boston: Houghton-Mifflin Company, 1989, 1991.

Don Dinkmeyer and Lewis E. Losoncy. *The Encouragement Book: Becoming a Positive Person*. Englewood Cliffs, NJ: Prentice-Hall, 1980.

Dale Carnegie. *How to Win Friends and Influence People*. New York: Simon and Schuster, 1936, 1964.

Alix Kirsta. *The Book of Stress Survival*. New York: Simon and Schuster, 1986.

The authors wish to thank the people who participated in the interviews for the book. Michael would like to thank Brett Saunders, Eric Saunders, Ammon Rost, Lisa Rost, and Lynn Todd. Anne would like to thank the McGannons, the Fowkes, and friends at the ALI at San Francisco State University.

The Publishers and authors wish to express thanks to those who reviewed earlier versions of the manuscript and provided helpful suggestions: Charles M. Browne, Gwen Thurston Joy, Tamara Swenson, Judy Boyle, Janis Oppie Smith, Nobuhiro Kumai, Julie Bradrick, Jackie Pels, Kevin Bergman, Shinsuke Suzuki, Dugie Cameron, Steve Martin, Hideki Komiyama, and Hiromi Tsuchiya.

Contents

UNIT 1. Glad to Meet You. **2**
   Let's Start: First Meetings
   Social World: What's Your Name?
   Skill Builders: Names, Addresses, & Phone
      Numbers
   Personal World: Talking About Names
   Conversation Strategies:
      1: SHOW INTEREST
      2: ASK FOR REPETITION

UNIT 2. Let's Talk About Names **8**
   Interview: Talking About Names
   Quiz: What's in a Name?
   Activity: What is Your Magic Number?

UNIT 3. What's Your Schedule? **10**
   Let's Start: Daily Routines
   Social World: Schedules
   Skill Builders: Times, Days, and Dates
   Personal World: I Can't Live Without It
   Conversation Strategies:
      3: REPEAT THE QUESTION
      4: THINK OUT LOUD

UNIT 4. Let's Talk About Lifestyles . . **16**
   Interview: Favorite Activities
   Quiz: Lifestyles
   Activity: Do You Have Too Much Stress?

UNIT 5. Thanks for Your Help **20**
   Let's Start: Buying Things
   Social World: Shopping Spree
   Skill Builders: Numbers and Prices
   Personal World: Shopping
   Conversation Strategies:
      5: CHECK IT OUT
      6: CONFIRM IT

UNIT 6. Let's Talk About Shopping . . **26**
   Interview: Shopping Habits
   Quiz: Shopping Talk
   Activity: Looking for a Bargain

UNIT 7. What Is She Like? **28**
   Let's Start: Describing Friends
   Social World: Describing People
   Skill Builders: Saying It Fast
   Personal World: Personalities
   Conversation Strategies:
      7: GIVE A SUMMARY
      8: ASK A SUMMARY QUESTION

UNIT 8. Let's Talk About People **34**
   Interview: Your Friends
   Quiz: A Picture Is Worth a Thousand Words
   Activity: Color Test

UNIT 9. I'm Getting Better **38**
   Let's Start: Thanking, Apologizing,
      Inviting
   Social World: Language Functions
   Skill Builders: Predicting a Response
   Personal World: A Second Language
   Conversation Strategies:
      9: SHOW AGREEMENT OR DISAGREEMENT
     10: SHOW SOMETHING IN COMMON

UNIT 10. Let's Talk About
      Languages. **44**
   Interview: Your Purpose for Learning English
   Quiz: Where Did That Come From?
   Activity: Survey: Are You a Good Language
      Learner?

UNIT 11. What Do You Do? **46**
Let's Start: Starting a Conversation
Social World: Getting to Know You
Skill Builders: Colloquial Expressions
Personal World: Making Friends
Conversation Strategies:
    11: ASK FOR EXAMPLES
    12: OFFER AN EXAMPLE

UNIT 12. Let's Talk About Making Friends **52**
Role Play: Getting to Know People
Quiz: The Personals
Activity: Making Friends—What the Professionals Say

UNIT 13. Sounds Like a Great Experience! **54**
Let's Start: Talking About Travel
Social World: A Great Experience
Skill Builders: Sequences
Personal World: A Memorable Place
Conversation Strategies:
    13: CHECK FOR UNDERSTANDING
    14: REPHRASE IT

UNIT 14. Let's Talk About Travel **60**
Interview: Visiting Places
Quiz: The First!
Activity: Sightseeing

UNIT 15. It's Important to Us **62**
Let's Start: Weekend Activities
Social World: Around the City
Skill Builders: Body Idioms
Personal World: Are You Typical?
Conversation Strategies:
    15: TAKE TIME TO THINK
    16: CHANGE THE QUESTION

UNIT 16. Let's Talk About Culture . . **68**
Interview: Ideas About Culture
Quiz: Our National Culture
Activity: Culture Test

UNIT 17. What Are You Planning to Do? **70**
Let's Start: Weekend Plans
Social World: Future Plans
Skill Builders: In Your Future
Personal World: Advances in the Future
Conversation Strategies:
    17: RESTATE THE IDEA
    18: SHOW THAT YOU UNDERSTAND

UNIT 18. Let's Talk About the Future **76**
Interview: Advice for the Future
Quiz: Advances in Our Past
Activity: Fortune Cookie Game

Tape Scripts **78**

Introduction

Keynote is a language course for students at the "false beginner" level who wish to activate their knowledge of English and develop their ability to understand and use the spoken language.

Keynote utilizes a unique approach to language practice: each unit is based on realistic samples of language use and authentic samples of spoken discourse.

The eighteen chapters of the book are grouped into pairs of units.

In the first unit of each pair (Units 1, 3, 5, etc.), students are exposed to realistic models of conversation and structured practice. In these units the students learn to comprehend language holistically and then to examine structural, functional, and strategic features of the language.

In the second unit of each pair (Units 2, 4, 6, etc.), students participate in a variety of activities and tasks that allow them to use the vocabulary, structures, functions, and strategies they have just practiced.

Keynote is accompanied by a set of **cassettes**. The cassettes provide models for several sections of the textbook (Conversation Samples and Conversation Strategy Examples) and input for listening tasks (Social World and Personal World sections). A **Teacher's Manual** is also available. The manual provides tape scripts, answer keys, and specific teaching suggestions to supplement the general suggestions given in this introduction.

Description of the Sections

Conversation

Each set of units has a **Conversation** section which provides a function for the students to practice in different situations. The students are to listen to the sample conversation according to the instructions given.

After they listen to the models, the students begin **Pair Practice**. This section provides conversation frames in which the students substitute or add information supplied, or provide personal information.

Social World

Each set of units also contains selective listening tasks, which appear in the **Social World** section. This section provides functional tasks, such as filling out forms and schedules, that are part of our social world. Realistic samples of language are presented from which the students extract only the necessary information.

Skill Builders

This section provides intensive practice with specific listening points. Topics, vocabulary, and structures from the previous sections are recycled and the "skill builder" exercises reinforce what the students have practiced. Because the section isolates specific listening problems, students will find their listening skills improving as they work with this section.

Personal World

This section introduces informal models of spoken English, in which fluent speakers talk about questions related to the theme of the unit, often in interesting and surprising ways. Although the students are exposed to realistic discourse, the exercises in this section are clearly structured (with pre-listening and successive listening exercises) so that the students can comprehend the gist of what each speaker is saying.

Conversation Strategies

One of the unique features of **Keynote** is the introduction of clear strategies that the students can *identify* in the conversation sample and also *use* in their own speech. Each set of units introduces one or two strategies, with examples (on tape) and opportunities for extended practice.

Let's Talk

The second unit of each pair of units is entitled "Let's Talk." This unit continues the theme of the previous unit, providing the students with three separate activities for **pair work** and **small group** exchanges.

Interview or Role Play

This is a "free conversation" activity that provides a basic structure for the students to work in pairs. Topics, questions, and conversation strategies from the previous unit are used to encourage immediate application of what the students have just learned.

Quiz

This is an "outcome-oriented" pair or small-group activity. The quiz is meant to be a problem-solving activity (not a test in which the students are expected to know the answers in advance). By working together, using clues in the quiz and a process of elimination, they can usually solve the puzzle.

Most quizzes have a follow-up expansion activity written in the student book.

Activity

This is an "open-ended" pair or small-group activity which encourages discussion and expansion of a thematic area. Each activity follows a clear set of steps, so that all students can be involved, and a follow-up task to allow for an exchange of opinions and ideas.

Tape Scripts

The appendix contains the tape scripts for the Social World, Skill Builders, and Personal World sections. (The appendix contains only the dialogues and exercise material; the narration sections appear on the student pages.) For best results, the tape scripts should be reviewed by the students only after they have listened to the tape and have attempted the textbook exercises.

Timing of the Units

Keynote provides material for 30 class periods of 60-90 minutes. Each of the introduction units (1, 3, 5, 7, 9, 11, 13, 15, 17) requires approximately two full class periods to cover. Each of the **Let's Talk** units requires a minimum of one full class period, with additional time required if the expansion and discussion options are used.

The Teacher's Manual provides additional suggestions on timing of the unit activities.

UNIT 1 Glad to Meet You . . .

Let's Start

CONVERSATIONS

Listen to the conversations two times.
First listen without looking at the book. Then listen as you read.

1

Hi. Are you in this class?
Hi, my name's Beth.
Glad to meet you too, Brian.

Yes, I am. My name's Brian.
Glad to meet you, Beth.

2

Are you new here?
Hi, Laura. I'm Mark Miller.
Nice to meet you too, Laura.

Yes, I am. My name's Laura Sanchez.
Nice to meet you, Mark.

3

Do you live around here?
Hi, my name's Tina Nakamura.
Nice to meet you too, Pam.

Yes, I do. My name's Pam Forrest.
Nice to meet you, Tina.

Pair Practice

Now work in pairs.
Practice these conversations.

1

Hi. _____ _____ in this class?
Hi, my name's _____.
Glad to _____ _____ too, _____.

Yes, __ ____. My name's _____.
Glad to meet you, _____.

2

Do you _____ in this office?
Hi, _____, I'm _____ _____.
Nice to _____ _____ too, _____.

Yes, __ ____. My name's _____ _____.
Nice to meet you, _____.

3

Do you _____ around here?
Hi, my name's _____ _____.
Nice to _____ _____ too, _____.

Yes, __ ____. My name's _____ _____.
Nice to meet you, _____.

UNIT ONE 3

Social World

What's Your Name?

Listen and fill out these forms.

MILTON COLLEGE
STUDENT IDENTIFICATION CARD
Application Form

Name: _____

Address: _____

_____

Phone Number: _____

Social Security Number: _____

MOVIE NIGHT VIDEO RENTALS
MEMBERSHIP APPLICATION

Name: _____

Address: _____

_____

Phone Number: (_____) _____

Driver License Number: _____A178462_____

ID NUMBER: 24-33359-98070

Skill Builders

Names, Addresses, and Phone Numbers

ON TAPE

Names

Listen. Circle the correct name.

1. Carol Tanaka — Carol Tamura
2. Andre Thomas — Andre Thompson
3. Anna Hinson — Anna Timson
4. Sammy Martin — Sammy Martinez
5. Sue Wang — Sue Wong

Addresses

Listen. Circle the correct address.

6. 201 First Street — 2001 First Street
7. 15 Hall Street — 50 Hall Street
8. 1600 Penn Avenue, Apartment C — 1660 Penn Avenue, Apartment D
9. 1717 Whitehall, Room 201 — 1770 Whitehall, Room 102
10. Honolulu, Hawaii 99144 — Honolulu, Hawaii 91944

Telephone Numbers

Listen. Circle the correct phone numbers.

11. 883-2222 — 883-2244
12. 445-9810 — 445-8901
13. 224-7661 — 244-6771
14. (213) 662-0905 — (213) 622-0905
15. (617) 228-6524 — (617) 328-5642

UNIT ONE

Personal World — **Talking About Names**

FOCUS

Write your first name and family name on the lines.

Your name: _____ _____
(FIRST NAME)   (FAMILY NAME)

First Listening...

First read each question. Listen to the conversations. Then circle the correct answer.

1

What is his first name?
- Mike
- Mickey
- Michael

What is his family name?
- Parker
- Mantle
- Harper

2

What is her first name?
- Katherine
- Rose
- Kate

What is her family name?
- Long
- Roslin
- Lang

3

What is his first name?
- Stan
- Edward
- Sam

What is his family name?
- Clemens
- Edwards
- Rider

Second Listening...

Read each of these sentences. Listen again.
Then choose a, b, c, d, e, f, or g to complete each sentence.

1. Mickey was named after _____.
2. Katherine was named after _____.
3. Sam was named after _____.

a. her mother
b. her grandmother
c. her father
d. her grandfather
e. a famous writer
f. a football player
g. a baseball player

6 UNIT ONE

Conversation Strategies

1: SHOW INTEREST

Show interest in your partner's information.

ON TAPE — EXAMPLES

- My name's Katherine Jamison.
  Oh, that's a nice name.

- My name's Abraham Lincoln Finch.
  That's an interesting name.

- My name's Nikita Nkrumah.
  Oh, that's an unusual name.

Make short conversations.

1. What's your first name?
   It's _____.
   Oh, that's a (an) _____ name.

2. What's your family name?
   It's _____.
   Oh, that's a _____ name.

3. What's your mother's name?
   It's _____.
   Oh, that's a _____ name.

4. What's your father's name?
   It's _____.
   Oh, that's a _____ name.

2: ASK FOR REPETITION

If you don't hear correctly, ask your partner to say it again.

ON TAPE — EXAMPLES

- Hello, I'm Rudy Smith.
  I'm sorry, what's your first name again?

- Hi. I'm Mary Parazinski.
  I'm sorry, what's your family name again?

- My address is 1224 East Meadow Street.
  I'm sorry, what's your address again?

Make short conversations.

1. What's your full name?
   It's _____.
   I'm sorry, what's ____ ____ ____ again?

2. What's your address?
   It's _____.
   I'm sorry, what's _____ _____ again?

3. What's your phone number?
   It's _____.
   I'm sorry, what's ____ ____ ____ again?

4. When's your birthday?
   It's _____.
   I'm sorry, when's _____ _____ again?

UNIT ONE   7

UNIT 2

Let's Talk About Names

Interview

Work with a partner. First answer these questions. Write your answers in Column 1. Then ask your partner the questions. Write down your partner's answers in Column 2.

Now change roles. Your partner will ask the questions.

Remember to use the Conversation Strategies on page 7.

	COLUMN 1 (YOU)	COLUMN 2 (YOUR PARTNER)
1. What is your full name?	_____	_____
2. Do you have a nickname? What is it?	_____	_____
3. How was your name chosen? Were you named after someone?	_____	_____
4. Does your name have a special meaning?	_____	_____

Quiz

What's in a Name?

This is a match game. Work with a partner.
Partner A reads the items in the CLUES column.
Partner B finds the answers in the NAMES column.
When you finish, check your answers at the bottom of the page.

CLUES

1. One of the most popular American girls' names in 1990
2. The real name of the American writer Mark Twain
3. Pop star Madonna's family name
4. The five most common family names in the U.S.
5. This name means "red" in Spanish.
6. The initials of American President Kennedy
7. A common Japanese girl's name. It means "child of autumn."
8. This name means "good luck" in Latin.
9. The nickname of Earvin Johnson, the American basketball star
10. The nickname of a famous Brazilian soccer star

NAMES

Carmen
Ciccone
Felicia (for females), Felix (for males)
Jennifer
JFK
Akiko
Magic
Pele
Samuel Clemens
Smith, Johnson, Williams, Brown, Jones

Answer Key

1. Jennifer, 2. Samuel Clemens, 3. Ciccone, 4. (Smith, Johnson, Williams, Brown, Jones), 5. Carmen, 6. JFK, 7. Akiko, 8. Felicia/Felix, 9. Magic, 10. Pele

On Your Own

Make your own quiz. Write down 4 clues. Read them to your partner. Can your partner guess the name?

CLUES	NAMES
_____	_____
_____	_____
_____	_____
_____	_____

Activity: What Is Your Magic Number?

Steps

1. Write out your full name. This means, the name you use when someone asks you: "What is your full name?"

___ = _____

2. Count the numbers for each letter in your name. (Look at the chart.) Add the numbers.

   For example,
   John Smith = 1 + 7 + 5 + 5 + 3 + 4 + 1 + 4 + 5 = 35

3. Separate this number and add the digits together.
   (Example: 35 = 3 + 5 = 8)

   This is your magic number.
   Your magic number shows your "strong point."

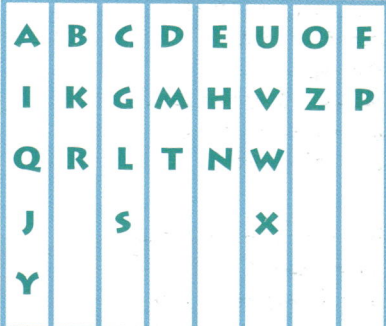

1	2	3	4	5	6	7	8
A	B	C	D	E	U	O	F
I	K	G	M	H	V	Z	P
Q	R	L	T	N	W		
J		S			X		
Y							

Follow Up

Work in a group of four. Ask your partners these questions:

What is your magic number?
What does it mean?
Does your magic number fit you?
Why or why not?

STRONG POINTS

1. Action -- you are able to do things, to take action
2. Fairness -- you see what is fair for everyone
3. Imagination -- you can see hidden ideas and answers
4. Basic truths -- you use your deeper principles to guide you
5. Adventure -- you like to take risks
6. Dependability -- you are able to trust and be trusted
7. Intellect -- you use your mind to think through difficulties
8. Toughness -- you stick with your ideas and principles

	Magic Number?	Meaning?	Does it fit?
NAME _____	_____	_____	_____
NAME _____	_____	_____	_____
NAME _____	_____	_____	_____

UNIT 3

Let's Start

What's Your Schedule?

CONVERSATIONS

Listen to the conversations two times.
First listen without looking at the book. Then listen as you read.

1

What time do you usually get up?
And what time do you leave for work?

*I usually get up at 6:30.
I leave the house about 7:45.*

2

When do you usually eat lunch?
What do you usually eat?

*Eat lunch? Usually at 12:30.
I usually eat a sandwich and some fruit.*

3

What do you usually do in the evening?
How about on the weekend?

*I usually watch TV or read a book.
On the weekend I usually go out
with friends.*

Pair Practice

**Now work in pairs.
Complete these questions.**

_____ _____ do you usually get up?

What time do you usually leave for _____ ?

When _____ _____ usually eat lunch?

____ ____ ____ ____ ____ in the evening?

What do you usually ____ on the weekend?

Write two more questions.

_____?

_____?

**Now ask your partner about his or her schedule.
Write your partner's activities in the schedule below.**

_____'S SCHEDULE
(PARTNER'S NAME)

6:00 a.m.
7:00 a.m.
8:00 a.m.
9:00 a.m.
10:00 a.m.
11:00 a.m.
12:00 noon
1:00 p.m.
2:00 p.m.
3:00 p.m.

4:00 p.m.
5:00 p.m.
6:00 p.m.
7:00 p.m.
8:00 p.m.
9:00 p.m.
10:00 p.m.
11:00 p.m.
12:00 midnight

Weekend Activities

UNIT THREE

Social World

Schedules

ON TAPE

Listen to the conversations.
Then complete the schedules with activities, names, and times.

1 Sue's Schedule

ACTIVITIES

go to class,
meet Sam for lunch,
work in the library,
meet Ted

MONDAY			
7		1	
8		2	
9		3	
10		4	
11		5	
12		6	

2 David's Schedule

ACTIVITIES

take a karate lesson,
go to Karen and Bill's wedding,
play tennis,
go to the movies with Kathy

	Saturday	Sunday
morning		
afternoon		

12 UNIT THREE

Skill Builders

Times, Days, and Dates

ON TAPE

Times

Listen. Circle the correct time.

1.	1:15	1:50
2.	2:13	2:30
3.	12:20	12:25
4.	4:00	5:00
5.	5:15	9:15
6.	8:40 a.m.	8:40 p.m.
7.	6:30 a.m.	6:30 p.m.
8.	11:00 a.m.	1:00 p.m.
9.	7:00 a.m.	7:00 p.m.
10.	10:00 a.m.	10:00 p.m.

Days and Dates

Listen. Circle the correct day or date.

11.	Tuesday	Thursday
12.	Saturday	Sunday
13.	Sunday	Monday
14.	Friday, the 15th	Friday, the 17th
15.	Wednesday, the 21st	Wednesday, the 23rd
16.	Tuesday, the 7th	Tuesday, the 17th
17.	June 20th	June 25th
18.	December 10th	December 12th
19.	May 13th	May 30th
20.	August 4th	August 14th

UNIT THREE

Personal World

I Can't Live Without It

FOCUS

Read this list. Which 3 things are most important in your daily life?
Write 1, 2, 3 next to your choices.

- ☐ a television
- ☐ a telephone
- ☐ a coffee maker
- ☐ a CD player
- ☐ a bicycle
- ☐ a computer
- ☐ (recorder)
- ☐ a refrigerator
- ☐ other _____ WHAT?

First Listening ...
ON TAPE

Listen to the conversations.
Which object do these people use every day?
Complete each sentence.

1. Mark uses _____ every day.

2. Anna uses _____ every day.

3. Sue uses _____ every day.

My Favorite Place

FOCUS

Which room in your house or apartment do you like the most?
Make a (✓) next to your favorite room.

☐ the living room   ☐ the bedroom   ☐ the kitchen   ☐ the study (or study room)   ☐ other _____

First Listening ...
ON TAPE

Listen to the conversations.
Which room does each person use most often?
Complete each sentence.

1. Marie uses _____ most often.

2. Atsushi uses _____ most often.

3. Lily uses _____ most often.

Second Listening ...

Listen again.
What do they do in their favorite rooms?
Complete each sentence.

1. Marie spends a lot of time _____.

2. Atsushi spends most of his time _____.

3. Lily spends a lot of time _____.

14 UNIT THREE

Conversation Strategies

3: REPEAT THE QUESTION

Do this when you need time to think.

EXAMPLES (ON TAPE)

- What's your favorite room?
  What's <u>my</u> favorite room?
  I guess it's my bedroom.

- What item is most important to you?
  What item is most important to <u>me</u>?
  Probably my computer.

Make short conversations.

1. A: What time do you get up?
   B: *What time do I get up?*
   I usually get up at _____.

2. A: What do you eat for breakfast?
   B: *What do I ____ __ _____?*
   I usually ____ ____ ____.

3. A: When do you get home from work? (or school?)
   B: _____?
   _____.

4. A: When do you go to bed?
   B: _____?
   _____.

4: THINK OUT LOUD

Do this to show that you understand the question.

EXAMPLES (ON TAPE)

- What's your favorite room?
  Hmm . . .
  I guess it's the family room.

- What item is most important to you?
  Let me think.
  Maybe my bicycle.

Make short conversations.

1. A: What's your favorite room?
   B: Hmm . . . _____.

2. A: What's your favorite food?
   B: Let me think . . . _____.

3. A: What's your favorite school subject?
   B: _____.

4. A: Who is your favorite teacher?
   B: _____.

UNIT THREE

UNIT 4

Let's Talk About Lifestyles

Interview

Work with a partner. First answer these questions. Write your answers in Column 1. Then ask your partner the questions. Write down your partner's answers in Column 2.

Remember to use the Conversation Strategies on page 15.

	COLUMN 1 (YOU)	COLUMN 2 (YOUR PARTNER)
1. What three items are very important to you?	1. _____	_____
	2. _____	_____
	3. _____	_____
2. Why are they important?	_____	_____
3. What are your favorite activities at home?	_____	_____
4. What is one free time activity you do outside your home?	_____	_____

Now change roles. Your partner will ask the questions.

16　□　UNIT FOUR

Quiz: Lifestyles

Work with a partner.

Partner A reads 1, 3, 5.
Partner B finds the answer (a - h).

Partner B reads 2, 4, 6.
Partner A finds the answer (a - h).

Check your answers.

LIFESTYLES

1. My day starts pretty early, about 6:30. I get up with the kids and fix breakfast for everybody. After that I take my oldest son to school and then do some shopping on the way home.

2. I'm up early, usually by 6:00. First thing, I turn on my computer and check the markets in Japan and London. Then I go to the kitchen and read the Wall Street Journal while I drink a cup of coffee. I get to the office by 7:30.

3. I usually get up at dawn, about 5:30 or 6:00. . . . I drink a glass of orange juice and then go out jogging on the beach. After I jog, I usually spend the morning reading through new screenplays and movie scripts.

4. I get up around 4:30 because I have to be at work by 6:00 am. We usually meet with the producer first and plan our news stories for the day. Then the camera operator and I go out and get our stories for the evening broadcast.

5. I never get up before 11 or 12. That's because I always work nights. We usually play at a club until 1 or 2 in the morning. During the afternoon, we usually get together and practice for two or three hours.

6. I always try to sleep eight hours a night, then I get up around 7:30. Before breakfast, I work out at the gym, lifting weights. Then it's practice all afternoon, 6 days a week. We usually play our games in the evenings.

OCCUPATIONS

a. an actor or actress
b. a politician
c. a stockbroker
d. a student
e. a parent
f. a news reporter
g. a musician
h. a professional athlete

Answer Key 1-e, 2-c, 3-a, 4-f, 5-g, 6-h.

Activity: Do You Have Too Much Stress?

Stress is stimulationn of the nervous system in our bodies. <u>Some</u> stress is good for our health because stress creates energy in the body. But <u>too much</u> stress is bad for us.

How much stress is too much? Some doctors try to estimate "stress" by counting "stress points" for our lifestyle. Take this test to see how much daily stress you have.

Work with a partner.

Steps

1. Read each question to your partner. Circle your partner's answer. (Remember: Be honest!)
2. Count the total "stress points."
3. Change roles. Answer your partner's questions. Count the total "stress points."
4. Look at the table. Do you have too much stress?

Your View of Yourself

1. Do you feel you have an interesting personality?	Yes (-2 points)	No (5 points)	_____
2. Is it hard for you to talk about your problems?	Yes (3 points)	No (0 points)	_____
3. Do you often worry about your job in the future?	Yes (4 points)	No (0 points)	_____
4. Do you try to give more than 100% in all of your activities?	Yes (5 points)	No (0 points)	_____

Your "Living Space"

1. Do you feel your home is too small for you?	Yes (4 points)	No (0 points)	_____
2. Do you have enough privacy?	Yes (-2 points)	No (3 points)	_____
3. Is it hard for you to relax at home?	Yes (5 points)	No (0 points)	_____
4. Do you spend a lot of time in crowded trains or in heavy traffic?	Yes (4 points)	No (-1 point)	_____

Your Relationships

1. Are you able to relax with your friends?	Yes (-2 points)	No (5 points)	_____
2. Do you feel you do too much for other people?	Yes (3 points)	No (0 points)	_____
3. Is it difficult for you to find a permanent love relationship?	Yes (4 points)	No (0 points)	_____
4. Do you have to spend a lot of time with people you don't like?	Yes (5 points)	No (0 points)	_____

Your Job or School

1. Do you feel you are working too hard? — Yes (4 points) — No (0 points) _____
2. Are you bored with your job or school? — Yes (-2 points) — No (3 points) _____
3. Do you find it hard to talk to your boss or teacher? — Yes (5 points) — No (0 points) _____
4. Do you have to do many things you don't like? — Yes (4 points) — No (-1 point) _____

Your Time

1. Do you often try to do many things at the same time? — Yes (-2 points) — No (5 points) _____
2. Are you always in a hurry? — Yes (3 points) — No (0 points) _____
3. Do you regularly take breaks during your work time? — Yes (4 points) — No (0 points) _____
4. Do you sleep less than 6 hours a night? — Yes (5 points) — No (0 points) _____

Stress Table

- 0 - 20 Not enough stress in your life--you probably need <u>more</u> excitement.
- 21 - 40 Moderate stress--you probably can handle your stress well.
- 41 - 60 A lot of stress in your life--you need to relax more.
- 61 - 79 Too much stress! You should be careful to take care of yourself.

Follow Up

Fill in the table.

Partner's Name	Score	Meaning	Does It Fit?
_____	____	_____	____

Now ask your partner these questions:

Do you agree with your score?
How do you deal with stress?
Do you have any advice for me?

UNIT FOUR 19

UNIT 5

Thanks for Your Help . . .

Let's Start

CONVERSATION

First listen as you read the conversation.
Then repeat the conversation.

ON TAPE

Excuse me. I'm looking for a coffee maker.

How much are they?

Oh, I see. Thanks for the information.

Well, we have two models on sale:
a Philips and a General Electric.

The Philips is $79 and the General Electric is $99.

You're welcome.

Pair Practice

Work in pairs.
Make new conversations like the one above.

1
Partner A: You're looking for some inexpensive running shoes.
Partner B: You have two styles on sale: the Pacers, $45, and the Nino Nakanos, $65

Excuse me. I'm looking for _____.

How much are they?

Oh, I see. Thanks for the information.

Well, we have two styles:
_____ and _____.

The _____ are $_____ and the _____ are $_____.

You're welcome.

20 UNIT FIVE

2 Partner A: You're looking for a personal computer.
   Partner B: You have two models: the Advance, $1700; the LDF, $2300

Excuse me. I'm looking for _____.

How much are they?

Oh, I see. Thanks for the information.

Well, we have two models: _____ and _____.

The _____ is $___ and the _____ is $___.

You're welcome.

3 Partner A: You're looking for a raincoat.
   Partner B: You have two styles: the London Fog, $150; the Burberry, $250

Excuse me. I'm looking for _____.

How much are they?

Oh, I see. Thanks for the information.

Well, we have two styles: _____ and _____.

The _____ is $___ and the _____ is $___.

You're welcome.

4 Partner A: You're looking for a book about the Olympic Games.
   Partner B: You have two books: The Olympics, Past and Present, $9
                                    The Guidebook to the Olympics, $20

Excuse me. I'm looking for _____.

How much are they?

Oh, I see. Thanks for the information.

Well, we have two books: _____ and _____.

The _____ is $___ and the _____ is $___.

You're welcome.

UNIT FIVE   21

Social World

Shopping Spree

Listen. Which item are they talking about? Put the number of the conversation next to the item.

☐ a house ☐ a sweater ☐ a car ☐ a book ☐ a fax machine ☐ a computer ☐ a camera

The Right Price

Listen and write the price for each item.

1. Hardy's Student Dictionary _____
   New Translator's Dictionary _____

2. 1989 Cyprus _____
   1991 Mantra _____

3. a desk _____
   a lamp _____
   a bookshelf _____

4. a sweater _____
   jeans _____
   a jacket _____

Skill Builders

Numbers and Prices

Listen. Circle the correct number or price.

1.	12	20	21	11.	$39.95	$35.59
2.	15	115	150	12.	$5.50	$5.15
3.	14	42	40	13.	$124.77	$224.70
4.	101	1,001	110	14.	$808	$880
5.	27	37	47	15.	$2,600	$26
6.	3,200	2,300	3,020	16.	$7,600	▶ ¥1 million	¥2 million (Japan)
7.	1,150	11,500	11,050	17.	$409	▶ ₩313,000	₩330,000 (Korea)
8.	55,000	55,500	55,550	18.	$7,600	▶ CAN$19,000	CAN$9,000 (Canada)
9.	125,000	129,000	199,000	19.	$9950	▶ DM15,600	DM56,000 (Germany)
10.	16,000	6,000	1,600	20.	$4 million	▶ NT 89 million	NT 98 million (Taiwan)

22   UNIT FIVE

Personal World — **Shopping**

FOCUS

What was the last thing you bought? Check one.

☐ food or drink?   ☐ clothes?   ☐ a newspaper, magazine, or book?

☐ furniture or something for your house?   ☐ something else?

What did you buy? _____

First Listening . . .

Listen to the conversations.
What was the last thing each person bought? Complete each sentence.

1

2

3

David bought _____   Elaine bought _____   Taka bought _____

Second Listening . . .

Listen again.
Circle one expression to describe what each person bought.

1 David	**2** Elaine	**3** Taka
light brown	big	easy to use
dark brown	comfortable	easy to carry
light gray	expensive	fun
dark gray	fast	noisy

UNIT FIVE   23

Clothes

FOCUS

What's your favorite item of clothing?

_____

What are your favorite colors for your clothes?

_____

First Listening...

Listen to the conversations.
What clothes does each person wear most often? Complete each sentence.

1 David wears _____

2 Elaine wears _____

3 Taka wears _____

Second Listening...

Listen again.
What colors do they wear most often? Complete each sentence.

1 David likes to wear _____

2 Elaine likes to wear _____

3 Taka likes to wear _____

UNIT FIVE

Conversation Strategies

5: CHECK IT OUT

When your partner's question is not clear, ask for clarification.

ON TAPE EXAMPLES

- What was the last thing you bought?
  The last thing I bought? What do you mean?

- What was the last big thing you bought?
  I'm not sure what you mean.

Make short conversations.

Now practice this strategy in new conversations like this:

What is **the best kind of clothes?**
***The best kind of clothes?** What do you mean?*
I mean, the best clothes for travelling.
Oh, the best clothes for travelling are jeans and comfortable shoes. . . .

1. What is the best kind of clothes?
   The _____? What do you mean?
   I mean, clothes for school.
   Oh, _____.

2. Where do you usually shop for music?
   Shop for music? What _____?
   I mean, for tapes and CDs.
   _____

3. How much do you usually spend?
   How much do I usually spend? What _____?
   I mean, for entertainment.
   _____

6: CONFIRM IT

Try this to check if your partner understands your meaning.

ON TAPE EXAMPLES

- What was the last thing you bought over $100?
  I guess . . . it was a suit. An Armani suit.
  Do you know that designer?

- What was the last movie you saw?
  Hmm . . . it was Silence of the Lambs.
  Do you know that movie?

Make short conversations.

Now practice this strategy in new conversations like this:

Who's your favorite singer?
I guess . . . Mariah Carey.
Do you know that singer?

1. Who's your favorite musical group?
   I guess . . . _____.
   _____?

2. What was the last movie you saw?
   Hmm . . . _____.
   _____?

3. What was the last book you read?
   _____.
   _____?

4. Write your own:

   _____

   _____

UNIT 6

Let's Talk About Shopping

Interview

Work with a partner. Write your answers. Ask your partner. Write down your partner's answers.

Remember to use the Conversation Strategies on page 25.

	COLUMN 1 (YOU)	COLUMN 2 (YOUR PARTNER)
1. Where do you buy most of your food?	_____	_____
clothes?	_____	_____
"fun items"? (CDs, comic books, magazines, etc.)	_____	_____
2. What clothes do you wear most often?	_____	_____
What colors do you like to wear?	_____	_____
What colors do you hate to wear?	_____	_____

Quiz

Shopping Talk Work with a partner. Put the conversations together. When you finish, check your answers at the bottom of the page.

1. Can I help you?
2. What size do you wear?
3. What color are you looking for?
4. Do you have this in a smaller size?
5. Will that be cash or charge?
6. Where is the shoe department, please?
7. Does this blouse come in other colors?
8. Could I try these on please?
9. Will there be anything else?

a. Certainly. The dressing rooms are over here.
b. No, thanks. I'm just looking.
c. No, I'm sorry, that's the only size.
d. Size 10.
e. Charge, please. American Express.
f. It comes in white, pink or blue.
g. Black or gray.
h. It's on the third floor.
i. No, thank you. That's all.

Answer Key 1-b, 2-d, 3-g, 4-c, 5-e, 6-h, 7-f, 8-a, 9-i

Now look at the situations. Can you remember what they are saying?

- Can I ____?
- No, thanks. I'm ____.
- Could I try these on please?
- Certainly. The ____ are over here.
- ... What ____ do you wear?
- Size 10.
- Do you ____ ____ in a smaller size?
- No, I'm sorry, that's the ____.
- ____ shoe department, please?
- It's on the third floor.
- ____ ____ ?
- Charge, please. American Express.
- Does this blouse come in ____ ?
- It comes in ____.
- What color are you ____ ?
- Will there be anything else?
- No, ____.

Activity

Looking for a Bargain   Work with a partner.

Steps
1. Look at the items. Write the prices for them in your country.
2. Compare these prices with the prices in the United States. (Convert the US prices to your currency.)
3. Which items are more expensive in your country?

Items	Current Price in the U.S. USA Price 1995 Averages	Price in Your Country	Conversion in Dollars	More? > Less? < Same? =
1. a pair of Levi's jeans	$55			
2. a pair of athletic shoes (such as Nike Air®)	$85			
3. a personal stereo (such as Walkman®)	$175			
4. a movie ticket	$8.50			
5. one night rental of a video tape	$4			
6. a meal at a fast food restaurant (hamburger and a soft drink)	$6			
7. a cup of coffee in a restaurant	$2			
8. a soft drink from a vending machine	$1			
9. one month rent for a one-bedroom apartment in a large city	$500			
10. a morning newspaper	$.50			

Follow Up

**Work in a group of four.
Ask your partners these questions:**

What prices are rising quickly today in your country?
Has anything become cheaper in the last year? What?

UNIT SIX 27

UNIT 7 — What Is She Like?

Let's Start

CONVERSATIONS

Listen to the conversations two times. First listen without looking at the book. Then listen as you read.

1

Do you know my friend Tom?
He's about 25 . . . he's tall and has brown curly hair and a mustache.

I don't think so. What does he look like?

2

Do you know who Ted is?
He's wearing a green shirt, white pants and brown shoes.

No. What's he wearing?

Pair Practice — Appearance

Work in pairs. Choose one person and describe him or her. Say one sentence about: age, hair, height, and special features. Can your partner guess who it is?

VOCABULARY

Age
She's . . .
about 25
in her early twenties
in her late twenties

Hair
He has . . .
long hair
short hair
shoulder-length hair
curly hair
straight hair
dark hair
blond hair
gray hair

Height
She's . . .
very tall
tall
short
average height
about 180 cm
(6 feet)

Special Features
He/She . . .
has a nice smile
wears glasses
is good-looking

He . . .
has a beard
has a mustache
He's bald

28 UNIT SEVEN

Now change roles. Your partner will describe one person to you.
Can you guess who it is?

Clothes

Look at the picture again. Choose one person and describe what he or she is wearing. Can your partner guess which person it is?

VOCABULARY

Clothes

a long-sleeved shirt
a short-sleeved shirt
jeans
pants/slacks
shorts
a dress
a skirt
a blouse
a sweatshirt
a T-shirt
a suit
a tie
a sweater
a coat
a jacket
a hat
shoes
boots
sports shoes

Accessories

a belt
a watch
earrings
a necklace
a bracelet
a scarf
a purse
a backpack
a briefcase

Colors

white
red
orange
yellow
green
blue
purple
brown
black
gray
pink
silver
gold
light blue/green/brown
dark blue/green/brown

UNIT SEVEN 29

Social World

Describing People

ON TAPE

Listen. Who are these people?
Draw an arrow from each name to the correct person in the picture.

| James Parker | Maria Chacon | Laura Davis | Ken Matsumura | Alice Choy |

UNIT SEVEN

Skill Builders

Saying It Fast!

Changed Sounds
ON TAPE

In natural speech, some sounds <u>change</u> because of the words or sounds next to them. We do not always pronounce these sounds the way they are written.

You will hear two versions of a sentence. One will have <u>slow</u> pronunciation, the other will have <u>fast</u> pronunciation.
Listen and circle the correct word.

1. Do you <u>know</u> John?
   1st sentence: Do you know John?   a. (slow) fast
   2nd sentence: Do you know John?   b. slow (fast)

2. Did <u>you</u> meet Paula?
   1st sentence: a. slow fast
   2nd sentence: b. slow fast

3. No, who is <u>she</u>?
   1st sentence: a. slow fast
   2nd sentence: b. slow fast

4. You're <u>going</u> to like John.
   1st sentence: a. slow fast
   2nd sentence: b. slow fast

5. He's wearing a <u>nice</u> shirt.
   1st sentence: a. slow fast
   2nd sentence: b. slow fast

6. I want <u>you</u> to meet Alice.
   1st sentence: a. slow fast
   2nd sentence: b. slow fast

7. Did <u>you</u> see Maria?
   1st sentence: a. slow fast
   2nd sentence: b. slow fast

8. Do <u>you</u> see the tall slim woman?
   1st sentence: a. slow fast
   2nd sentence: b. slow fast

9. Yes, I'd <u>like</u> to meet her.
   1st sentence: a. slow fast
   2nd sentence: b. slow fast

10. Could <u>you</u> introduce us?
    1st sentence: a. slow fast
    2nd sentence: b. slow fast

Reduced Sounds

In natural speech, some words are not spoken completely; they are shortened or weakened. You hear only part of the word.

Listen to each sentence.
Write the missing words.

11. Have _____ seen _____?
12. _____ _____ _____ look like?
13. _____ _____ know.
14. Yes, I _____ _____.
15. She _____ _____ to dance.
16. She's _____ _____ _____ friends.
17. He _____ blond hair _____ glasses.
18. You're always talking _____ _____.
19. He's _____ a T-shirt _____ _____ tie!
20. Let's go talk _____ _____.

UNIT SEVEN   31

Personal World — **Personalities**

FOCUS
How do people describe your personality?
Write three words or expressions that people _____

_____ _____ _____

honest	funny	happy	cheerful	creative	boring
serious	active	interesting	friendly	intelligent	unfriendly
quiet	outgoing	talkative	nice	clever	

See JALT J Aug 94 P 73.

First Listening...

Listen to the conversations. How do other people describe these three speakers? Circle one word for each person.

1. People think Ingrid is: friendly   cool   energetic
2. People think Izumi is: creative   serious   quiet
3. People think Paul is: cheerful   intelligent honest

Second Listening...

Listen again. What is the reason for each description? Complete each sentence.

1. People think Ingrid is _____ because she _____.
2. People think Izumi is _____ because he _____.
3. People think Paul is _____ because he _____.

Friends

FOCUS
Who are your best friends? Write their names.
_____

Choose one of your friends. Write three words or expressions to describe his or her personality.

_____ _____ _____

First Listening...

Listen to these people describing their best friends. Circle all the words that you hear.

1. Lauren is: cheerful   nice   funny   calm   thoughtful
2. Erik is: funny   serious   clever   aggressive   lovable
3. Anatoly is: weird   interesting intelligent artistic   sociable

32 UNIT SEVEN

Conversation Strategies

7: GIVE A SUMMARY

Express your partner's meaning in your own words.

EXAMPLES ON TAPE

- Aki's really funny and we always have a good time together.
    It sounds like you really like him.
- I really like Paula. We do everything together.
    It sounds like she's your best friend.

Make short conversations.

Now practice this strategy in new conversations like this:

Tell me about your best friend.
   He's good at sports and always plays to win.
It sounds like he's very competitive.
   Yes, he is.

CHOOSE: interesting, popular, lazy, intelligent, funny, hard-working, serious

1. Tell me about your best friend.
   She's outgoing and she has lots of friends.
   It sounds like she's _____.
   _____.

2. Tell me about your sister.
   She's a good student; she always gets good grades.
   It sounds like she's _____.
   _____.

3. Write your own:
   _____.
   _____.
   _____.
   _____.

8: ASK A SUMMARY QUESTION

Ask about your partner's meaning in your own words.

EXAMPLES ON TAPE

- Young always makes people laugh.
    Do you mean she's funny?
- David and I go a lot of places together. I really like to spend time with him.
    Do you mean you always have a good time together?

Make short conversations.

Now practice this strategy in new conversations like this:

Tell me about your brother.
   He studies a lot and he always gets good grades.
Do you mean he's very academic?
   Yes, that's exactly what I mean.

1. Tell me about your best friend.
   She always tries new things.
   Do you mean she's _____?
   _____.

2. Tell me about your sister.
   She's a good musician; she listens to music a lot.
   Do you mean she's _____?
   _____.

3. Write your own:
   _____.
   _____.
   _____.
   _____.

UNIT SEVEN

UNIT 8

Let's Talk About People

Interview

Work with a partner.. Write your answers. Then ask your partner. Write down your partner's answers.

Remember to use the Conversation Strategies on page 33.

	COLUMN 1 (YOU)	COLUMN 2 (YOUR PARTNER)
1. Who is one of your good friends?	_____	_____
2. How did you become friends?	_____	_____
3. Why do you like him or her?	_____	_____
4. Who is the most interesting person you know?	_____	_____
5. Why is he or she so interesting?	_____	_____
6. How do you choose your friends?	_____	_____

Quiz

A Picture Is Worth a Thousand Words

Can you tell something about people just from their picture?

Work with a partner. Partner A reads the questions next to pictures 1, 3, and 5. Partner B decides which answer is correct. Partner B reads the questions next to pictures 2 and 4. Partner A decides which answer is correct. When you finish, check your answers at the bottom of the page.

Photo 1
1. Is his name Sam Hue or Yoshi Kono?
2. Is he single or married?
3. Is he 22 or 28 years old?
4. Is he an art student or a business student?
5. Is he talkative and outgoing or is he serious and quiet?

Photo 2
1. Is his name Larry Hill or Pierre LeConte?
2. Is he single, married, or divorced?
3. Is he 28, 38, or 48 years old?
4. Is he American, Canadian, or French?
5. Is he a scientist or a writer?

Photo 3
1. Is her name Shareen Foster or Mary Ann McMillan?
2. Is she a housewife or a designer?
3. Is she about 25 or about 30 years old?
4. Is she calm and relaxed or active and energetic?
5. Does she like to drive fast cars or read books?

Photo 4
1. Is his name Pietro Borelli or Peter Douglas?
2. Is he American, Italian, or British?
3. Is he a student or a tennis player?
4. Is he funny or serious?
5. Does he enjoy doing things outside or staying home?

Photo 5
1. Is her name Margaret Campbell or Ulrike Müller?
2. Is she from Canada or Austria?
3. Is she a happy person or an unhappy person?
4. Is she married or single?
5. Is she a chef, a tour guide, or a doctor?

Answer Key

1. His name is Sam Hue. He is from Hong Kong, but is now studying in Los Angeles. He's 22 years old, his major is dance. He is talkative and outgoing.
2. His name is Larry Hill. He is 38 years old. He was married for 10 years, but is now divorced. He lives in Seattle. He is an aerospace engineer.
3. Her name is Shareen Foster. She is 30 years old and works as a designer. She is energetic and she likes to drive fast cars.
4. His name is Peter Douglas. He is a tennis player from Great Britain. He is usually very funny and enjoys doing things outside.
5. Her name is Ulrike Müller. She is from Austria but she often works in Asia. She is a tour guide. She is single and she's a happy person.

On Your Own . . .

With your partner, think of three famous people. Complete the table.

Name: _____	Name: _____	Name: _____
Age: _____	Age: _____	Age: _____
Personality: _____	Personality: _____	Personality: _____
Interests: _____	Interests: _____	Interests: _____

UNIT EIGHT

Activity Color Test
Adapted from: Dorothee L. Mella, *The Language of Color*, Warner Books, 1988

What do your color preferences show about your personality? Take this test and find out!

Steps
1. Which of these colors do you *enjoy wearing*?
   Write the two colors in the "like most" column (#1) and (#2).
2. Which of these colors do you *avoid wearing*?
   Write the two colors in the "like least" column (#3) and (#4).
3. Find your characteristics in the Color Characteristics Table on the next page.
   Write the characteristics next to the colors you chose.
   Use your dictionary to find the meaning of words you don't know.

red   pink   orange   yellow   green

blue-green   light blue   dark blue   purple   brown

black   white   gray   silver   gold

Colors Table

LIKE MOST   **CHARACTERISTICS**

1. _____
2. _____

LIKE LEAST   **CHARACTERISTICS**

3. _____
4. _____

36 ☐ UNIT EIGHT

Color Characteristics Tables

Colors 1 and 2 -- Your strongest aspects

red	you like challenges; you have a lot of courage
pink	you are affectionate (you show love to others) and compassionate (you feel sympathy for others)
orange	you are active and organized
yellow	you are communicative; you enjoy being social
green	you are friendly; you enjoy giving to other people
blue-green	you are idealistic and faithful to your friends
light blue	you are creative (you have many original ideas) and perceptive (you notice many things)
dark blue	you are intelligent and responsible
purple	you are spiritual and noble (like a king or queen)
brown	you are honest and down-to-earth
black	you are strong-willed and independent
white	you are searching for answers and thinking about yourself
gray	you are stressed or overworked
silver	you are honorable and romantic
gold	you are successful and goal-oriented

Colors 3 and 4 -- Your weakest aspects

red	you sometimes can't control your temper; you become angry with yourself
pink	you sometimes feel too dependent on others
orange	you don't like to face your frustrations
yellow	you set very high expectations for yourself and occasionally feel you are not living up to them
green	you sometimes feel unlucky when you have a difficult experience
blue-green	you sometimes feel emotional stress and don't believe in your ability
light blue	you often feel mental stress because you don't play enough
dark blue	you often feel stress because you don't relax enough
purple	you often try to do things by yourself and don't trust other people enough
brown	you often worry; you sometimes work too hard because you are afraid you might fail
black	you sometimes avoid thinking deeply
white	you don't like to feel lonely so you avoid doing things by yourself
gray	you sometimes feel that other people don't respect you
silver	you sometimes feel that your friends won't trust you
gold	you feel you might lose success or financial rewards

Follow Up

Work with a partner. First guess your partner's colors.

PARTNER'S NAME	LIKES TO WEAR	AVOIDS WEARING

Check with your partner. Were your guesses correct?
Now ask your partner these questions:

Do you agree with the results of your color test?
Why do you think colors are important to people?

UNIT EIGHT

UNIT 9

I'm Getting Better . . .

Let's Start

CONVERSATIONS

ON TAPE — First listen as you read the conversations. Then repeat each conversation.

1 thanking

Wow, this is a nice gift.
Thanks a lot.

You're welcome.
I'm glad you like it.

2 apologizing

I'm sorry I was
late this morning.

That's OK.

3 asking for action

Would you mind opening
the window, please?

Sure, no problem.

4 asking permission

Is it OK if I use
your phone?

Of course, go ahead.

5 making suggestions

Hey, let's go to
a movie tonight.

Yeah, that sounds good.

6 inviting and refusing

Would you like to go
to a party tonight?

I'm sorry,
I can't tonight.

38 UNIT NINE

Pair Practice

**Work in pairs.
Make new conversations like the ones above.**

1 **Partner A: Thank your partner for the new watch.**

A: Thank you for the watch.
I really like it. _____.

B: You're _____.
I'm glad you _____.

2 **Partner A: Apologize because you couldn't come to the party last night.**

A: _____.

B: That's _____.

3 **Partner A: Ask your partner to turn on the light.**

A: _____.

B: _____, no problem.

4 **Partner A: Ask permission to borrow your partner's bicycle.**

A: _____.

B: Sure, go _____.

5 **Partner A: Make a suggestion to go to the beach this weekend.**

A: _____.

B: That sounds _____.

6 **Partner A: Invite your partner to go to a movie.**

A: _____.

B: I'm sorry, _____.

UNIT NINE 39

Social World

Language Functions

Each conversation uses one of the functions below. Listen and write the number of the conversation next to the correct function.

ON TAPE

A. THANKING _____

B. APOLOGIZING _____

C. ASKING FOR ACTION _____

D. ASKING PERMISSION _____

E. MAKING A SUGGESTION _____

F. INVITING AND REFUSING _____

G. INVITING AND ACCEPTING _____

40   UNIT NINE

Skill Builders

Predicting a Response

ON TAPE

Finding the Answer

Listen. What will the next speaker say? Circle the best answer.

1. a. See you soon.
   b. That's OK.
   c. I'm glad you like it.

2. a. Sure, no problem.
   b. Take care.
   c. Sure, go ahead.

3. a. Nice to meet you.
   b. That sounds good.
   c. Sure, go ahead.

4. a. I guess so.
   b. You're welcome.
   c. I'll meet you at school.

5. a. Yeah, I'll be there at 7.
   b. I'm glad you like it.
   c. That's OK.

6. a. OK, see you later.
   b. That sounds good.
   c. Let's go dancing.

7. a. You're welcome.
   b. Sure, go ahead..
   c. OK, bye.

8. a. Let's go out tonight.
   b. Oh, well. That's OK.
   c. I guess so. OK.

9. a. You're welcome.
   b. Hi, Rita.
   c. Let's dance.

10. a. I'll bring the drinks.
    b. I'm sorry about that.
    c. See you later.

Responding

Listen. What would you say next? Work with a partner. Write a short answer.

11. Yeah, bye.

12. Sorry, I've got to look after my sick kittens

13. Sure, How long will you be?

14. Hi Julie, Nice to meet you.

15. That's O.K. It's hard to predict.

16. About 8:15 or so.

17. Sorry, I don't lend CD's to anyone; I've lost too many

18. Yeah, I'd love to.

19. O.K, if you like

20. You're welcome. I'm glad you like it.

UNIT NINE   41

Personal World

A Second Language

FOCUS

In your opinion, what are the three most important world languages to learn? Write down three languages other than English.

_____ _____ _____

Many people study a second language at school. What kinds of activities do people do in most foreign language classes? Write down your ideas.

_____ _____ _____

Compare your answers with a partner.

First Listening...

Was it easy or difficult for them to learn a second language? Circle the answer.

1. very difficult   difficult   easy
2. very difficult   difficult   easy
3. very difficult   difficult   easy

Second Listening...

Listen again. What was the most difficult part to learn? Complete each sentence.

1. Anne: The most difficult part of learning French was _____.

2. Ken: The most difficult part of learning Japanese was _____.

3. Yumi: The most difficult part of learning English was _____.

A Good Language Learner

FOCUS

If someone wanted to learn to speak your language really well, what would you tell them to do? Write down three suggestions.

_____
_____
_____

First Listening...

According to each speaker, what makes a good language learner?

1. Beth: I think a good language learner is someone who _____.

2. Joe: I think a good language learner is someone who _____.

3. Marina: I think a good language learner is someone who _____.

42 UNIT NINE

Conversation Strategies

9: SHOW AGREEMENT OR DISAGREEMENT

Respond to your partner's opinion.

EXAMPLES

simple statements

- Ms. Harper's a great teacher.
  Yes, I think so too. OR *Really? I don't think so.*
  AGREEMENT   DISAGREEMENT

- This book is fun to use.
  Yeah, that's for sure. OR *I'm not sure about that.*
  AGREEMENT   DISAGREEMENT

negative statements

- English grammar isn't easy to understand.
  I don't think so either. OR *Really? I think it is.*
  AGREEMENT   DISAGREEMENT

- You can't learn a foreign language in your own country.
  Yeah, that's for sure. OR *Really? I think you can.*
  AGREEMENT   DISAGREEMENT

Practice the conversations.

1. A: Studying languages is fun.
   B: _____.
2. A: It's important to know a second language.
   B: _____.
3. A: It isn't easy to remember new vocabulary.
   B: _____.
4. A: Memorizing grammar rules doesn't help you speak better.
   B: _____.
5. Write your own:

   A. _____

   B. _____

10: SHOW SOMETHING IN COMMON

Show you have the same feeling or experience.

EXAMPLES

- I really like coming to this class.
  Do you? I do too.

- I enjoy our English conversation class.
  Really? I do too.

- I don't like to study for tests.
  Don't you? I don't either.

- I don't like talking in large groups.
  Really? I don't either.

Practice the conversations.

1. A: I enjoy reading books in English.
   B: _____.
2. A: I hate to practice English outside of class.
   B: _____.
3. A: I don't worry about making mistakes.
   B: _____.
4. A: I want to visit New Zealand someday.
   B: _____.
5. Write your own:

   A. _____

   B. _____

UNIT NINE 43

UNIT 10

Let's Talk About Languages

Interview

Work with a partner. Write your answers. Then ask your partner. Write down your partner's answers.

Remember to use the Conversation Strategies on page 43.

	COLUMN 1 (YOU)	COLUMN 2 (YOUR PARTNER)
1. What is your purpose for learning English?		
2. What's the most difficult part of this English class?		
3. What's the most enjoyable part of this English class?		
4. What makes a good language learner? Make a list:		

Quiz

Where Did That Come From?

Work with a partner.
Match the the words with the language they came from. Check your answers.

WORDS
1. circus   tradition   manufacture
2. kimono   futon   karate
3. alcohol   assassin   candy
4. coffee   kiosk   caviar
5. alphabet   theory   thermometer
6. champagne   ballet   boutique
7. know   house   night
8. tea   typhoon   ketchup

ORIGINAL LANGUAGES
a. Greek
b. French
c. Chinese
d. Latin
e. Arabic
f. Old German (Germanic)
g. Turkish
h. Japanese

French word + et = little ch sounds like sh (example: machine)

Germanic short words used every day (example: he, this)

Turkish many "k" sounds

Mandarin Chinese ta = great feng = wind; tsiap = sauce

Arabic al = the qand = sugar

Greek letters "phi" and "theta" are very common

Japanese consonant + vowel pattern: ka, ki, ku, ke, ko

Latin long (multi-syllable) words

Answer Key 1-d, 2-h, 3-e, 4-g, 5-a, 6-b, 7-f, 8-c

On Your Own

Now think of three English words—words you like or that are unusual. Check in an English dictionary. Can you find where these words came from?

_____   _____   _____

44   UNIT TEN

Activity

Survey: Are You a Good Language Learner?

Do you know what makes a good language learner? It's not only natural ability; it's also how you feel about learning and using the language.

Work with a partner.

Steps

1. Read each question to your partner. Circle your partner's answer. (Remember: Be honest!)
2. Change roles. Answer your partner's questions.
3. Now count up your partner's score: a answer = 0, b answer = 1, c answer = 2
4. Find out your score, then check it below. Are you a good language learner?

1. Do you get embarrassed when you make mistakes in English?
   a. yes, often   b. yes, sometimes   c. no, hardly ever

2. Do you avoid talking if you don't know how to express your ideas in English?
   a. yes, often   b. yes, sometimes   c. no, hardly ever

3. Do you usually try to find ways to use English outside of class?
   a. no, hardly ever   b. yes, sometimes   c. yes, often

4. If someone doesn't understand what you say, do you try to express your ideas in other words?
   a. no, hardly ever   b. yes, sometimes   c. yes, often

5. If someone doesn't understand what you say in English, do you usually say it in your native language?
   a. no, hardly ever   b. yes, sometimes   c. yes, often

6. Do you need to understand every word that you hear in English because you're not satisfied with only a general idea?
   a. yes, often   b. yes, sometimes   c. no, hardly ever

7. Do you practice English even when you're alone so you can be ready to communicate with others?
   a. no, hardly ever   b. yes, sometimes   c. yes, often

8. Do you listen to yourself when you speak to check your accuracy?
   a. no, hardly ever   b. yes, sometimes   c. yes, often

9. When people speak, do you have trouble understanding their meaning because you're trying to understand the grammar?
   a. yes, often   b. yes, sometimes   c. no, hardly ever

10. Do you dislike analyzing the grammar of language because it's not interesting?
    a. true   b. sometimes true   c. not true

11. Do you like English and are you interested in English-speaking cultures and their people?
    a. no, not really   b. yes, a little bit   c. yes, very much

12. Do you think that learning English will change your personality?
    a. yes, very much   b. yes, a little   c. no, not really

13. Do you try to learn outside of class without depending on the language textbook?
    a. no, hardly ever   b. yes, sometimes   c. yes, often

14. How long does it usually take successful language learners to "master" a new language?
    a. less than one year   b. one to three years   c. three to six years

Your Score: _____

0 - 10 points	**Be careful!** Some of your ideas may prevent you from learning a foreign language well.
11 - 21 points	**You're a very thoughtful language learner.** Some of your ideas will help you learn. Keep it up!
22+ points	**Congratulations!** You have an excellent attitude for language learning. **And you will probably be a successful language learner!**

Follow Up

Work with a partner. Ask your partner these questions.

Which of the survey questions is the most important? Why?

Which three of your answers would you like to change?

Now look at your partner's answers. Give your partner some advice.

You will be a better English speaker if _____.

UNIT TEN   45

UNIT 11 What Do You Do?

Let's Start

CONVERSATION

First listen as you read the conversation.
Then repeat the conversation.

Hello.
Are you travelling on business?
So am I. Who do you work for?

Hi.
Yes, I am.
I work for United Computer Systems.
I'm in sales. How about you? What do you do?

I'm an engineer.
At Transport Technologies.
Yeah, I like it there.

An engineer? Really? Where do you work?
Oh, that's a great company.

Pair Practice

Work in pairs. Make new conversations with the information below. Partner B must choose the correct answer.

1

greetings   something in common   introductions

Hi.

Hey, aren't you in my English class?

By the way, my name's Ken.

- Hello.
- Glad to meet you.

- I love English.
- Yes, I am.

- I'm Kip Larson.
- That's great.

46 □ UNIT ELEVEN

2   greetings   education   place you live

Hi, how's it going?	🕊	I'm Amy Jones. / Fine.
Do you go to Washington University?	🎓	Yes, I do. I'm a senior. / I do, too.
I have a friend there. Do you live in the dorms?	🏠	Yes, I live in Dorm A. / Yes, I have friends.

3   hobbies/interests   opinion   introductions

Do you play tennis?	🎾	Yes, I do. / How about you?
What do you think of this brand?	🙂	I think it's a nice day. / I think it's a good one.
By the way, my name's John.	✋	Really? So am I. / Hi, I'm Nancy.

4   introductions   hometown   occupation

Hi. Bob Reilly.	✋	Hi, Bob. I'm Nick O'Hara. / That's interesting.
Where are you from, (name)?	🏙	From Denver. / From my office.
Oh, I'm from (hometown). What do you do for a living?	💼	I like to play tennis. / I'm a computer programmer.

UNIT ELEVEN

| Social World | **Getting to Know You** |

Listen to these conversations. What topic do they talk about first? What topic do they talk about second? Write the correct number after each topic. In each conversation there are only two topics.

1. **AT A BUS STOP**
   - know the same person _____
   - weather _____
   - place you live _____
   - place you work _____

2. **AFTER CLASS**
   - education _____
   - greetings _____
   - introductions _____
   - opinions about the class _____

3. **AT A PARTY**
   - hometown _____
   - occupation _____
   - greetings _____
   - hobbies/interests _____

4. **AT THE OFFICE CAFETERIA**
   - weather _____
   - something in common _____
   - introductions _____
   - greetings _____

48 UNIT ELEVEN

Skill Builders

Colloquial Expressions

Sometimes in casual speech, people use colloquial expressions. Some colloquial expressions are not full grammatical forms.

ON TAPE

**Listen to these people talking.
What expressions do they use?
Put a check (✓) next to the correct one.**

1. ☐ Great party, isn't it?
   ✓ This is a great party, isn't it?

2. ☐ Yes, it is.
   ☐ Um-hmm, it is.

3. ☐ You a friend of Dave's?
   ☐ Are you a friend of Dave's?

4. ☐ Do you play soccer?
   ☐ You play soccer?

5. ☐ No, thanks.
   ☐ Hunh-unh, thanks.

6. ☐ It's a beautiful day, isn't it?
   ☐ Beautiful day, isn't it?

7. ☐ Want a drink?
   ☐ Do you want a drink?

8. ☐ How are you doing?
   ☐ How you doing?

9. ☐ You from around here?
   ☐ Are you from around here?

10. ☐ How about you?
    ☐ You?

Listen to the conversations. In the first line, you will hear the short form of a sentence (a colloquial expression). Write down the full form.

11. A: _____?
    B: No, I don't.

12. A: _____?
    B: Yeah, it really is.

13. A: _____?
    B: No thanks, I'm fine.

14. A: _____?
    B: Yeah, I do. Do you?

15. A: _____?
    B: Yeah, I am. You?

16. A: I'm from Atlanta. _____?
    B: I'm from Seattle.

17. A: _____?
    B: Yes, we work together.

18. A: _____?
    B: Good. And you?

19. A: _____?
    B: Yeah, it sure is.

20. A: _____?
    B: No, I'm a cashier.

Compare your answers with a partner.

UNIT ELEVEN   49

Personal World

Making Friends

FOCUS

Who is your oldest friend? _____

How long have you known him or her? _____

Who is your newest friend? _____

When did you meet him or her? _____

Is it easy for you to make friends? _____

Compare your answers with a partner.

First Listening...
ON TAPE

Listen to these people talking about making friends.
Is it easy for them to make friends? Circle the correct answer.

	(++)	(+)	(−)
1.	Yes, very easy.	Yes, sort of.	No, not really.
2.	Yes, very easy.	Yes, sort of.	No, not really.
3.	Yes, very easy.	Yes, sort of.	No, not really.

Meeting Friends

FOCUS

Where are some places to meet new friends?
Work with a partner and name five places.

_____ _____ _____ _____ _____ _____

First Listening...
ON TAPE

Listen to the conversations. How did these people meet most of their friends? Complete each sentence.

1. Julie meets most of her friends _____

2. Richard meets most of his friends _____

Second Listening...

Listen again.
Write down one example for each speaker.

1. Julie: people she has met -- example: _____

2. Richard: activities he does with friends -- example: _____

50　UNIT ELEVEN

Conversation Strategies

11: ASK FOR EXAMPLES

When you want more information, ask for examples.

EXAMPLES (ON TAPE)

- It's easy to make friends. I make friends everywhere.
  Can you give me an example?

- I can talk about lots of things with new friends.
  Like what?

12: OFFER AN EXAMPLE

When your partner wants more information, offer an example.

EXAMPLES (ON TAPE)

- A: It's easy to make friends. I make friends everywhere.

  B: Can you give me an example?

  A: Well, for example, at school, at work, in my neighborhood.

- A: I can talk about lots of things with new friends.

  B: Like what?

  A: Like music, sports, school, the news.

Make short conversations.

Now practice these strategies in new conversations like this:

A: I often make friends in unusual places.
　　　　B: Do you? **Can you give me an example?**
A: Well one time, for instance, I met some friends at a grocery store!
　　　　B: *Like who?*
A: *Like Martha.* She's my roommate now.

1. A: I've known most of my friends for a long time.
　　　　B: Oh, really? (ask for an example)
   A: (give an example)

2. A: I know a lot of famous people.
　　　　B: Do you? (ask for an example)
   A: (give an example)

3. A: Let's do something together after class today.
　　　　B: Okay. (ask for an example)
   A: (give an example)

4. Write your own:

   A: _____.

   　　B: _____

   A: _____.

UNIT ELEVEN　51

UNIT 12

Let's Talk About Making Friends

Role Play

Talk with two classmates for 2 minutes each. Try to mention 5 of these topics:

- greetings
- occupation
- education
- hometown
- hobbies/interests
- introductions
- weather
- place you work
- something in common
- person in common

Now can you remember? Try to fill in this table.

	CLASSMATE 1	CLASSMATE 2
name		
hometown		
occupation		
education		
hobbies/interests		
place you work		
something in common		
person in common		

Now check with your classmates. Is your information correct?

Quiz

The Personals

In many places, people who want to find a partner sometimes put an advertisement in the "Personals" section of the newspaper.

Work with a partner. Partner A reads 1 and 3. Partner B reads 5 - 8 to find a good match.

Partner B reads 2 and 4. Partner A reads 5 - 8 to find a good match. Check your answers.

1 I'm an eligible bachelor: 45 years old, active, healthy, very romantic, enjoys life. I'm looking for a special Asian woman, any age OK. I want a meaningful relationship based on respect and trust. My object is marriage! Please write to AB/218

5 I'm a quiet, thoughtful woman, 60 yrs young, 5'5". I lost my husband 5 years ago and I'm looking for a new companion. I enjoy cooking, watching TV, reading, and homelife. I am a good listener. And you? If you are kind, gentle, with a sense of humor, please write to me. No photo necessary. CD/106

2 I'm a good-natured gentleman, 48 years old. I enjoy skiing, waterskiing, and horseback riding. I am an animal lover--I have horses, dogs, and cats. I have a nice home and my own successful business. I am looking for a tall, athletic, playful, adventurous woman. Age is not important. Call. AB/332

3 I'm an honest, old-fashioned guy, 33. Educated, professional, energetic, I enjoy biking, racquetball, working out and traveling to new places. I don't smoke or drink. I'd like to meet an educated woman, 25-34, who enjoys culture, travel, dining out, and outdoor sports. Write to: AB/557

4 I'm a couch potato, 55 years old, 5'8", 210 lbs. I would like to meet healthy female couch potato who likes TV, junk food, cooking, reading and homelife. Please, no children, no travelers, no joggers. You don't have to be good-looking, just fun and interesting. Write to AB/601

6 I am an attractive, blue-eyed blonde professional looking for a rugged, outdoor man who likes dining out, theater, gardening, animals, outdoor sports, foreign travel, and adventure. You must be financially independent, 45-60. Write to CD/233

7 I am a warm-hearted, attractive Asian woman, slender 5'2", 37 years old. I'm intelligent, affectionate, fun-loving, but down-to-earth. I'm looking for a nice, attractive, tall American man, age 40-50. You must be honest and successful; no poor students. You should enjoy life to the fullest and be very romantic. Please send me a letter. CD812

8 I'm looking for one nice guy! I am a teacher, S, 5'10", 25 years old, no children. I love dancing, traveling, learning, and the outdoors. Let's share the good times together. Letters only please. Write to CD/794

Answer Key 1-7, 4-5, 2-6, 3-8

On Your Own
Write your own "Friend Personal." Post it on the blackboard.

Activity — Making Friends--What the Professionals Say

Look at the suggestions below on how to make friends. Can you find the <u>ten real</u> suggestions (from experts on making friends)? Work with a partner.

Steps
1. Read the sentences together out loud.
2. Decide if it is a "real" suggestion or not. Write + next to the sentences.
3. Compare with another pair. Then check your answers at the bottom.

☐ 1. Show other people that you are interested in them.
☐ 2. Invite people out for dinner at least once a week.
☐ 3. Buy people expensive presents.
☐ 4. Smile a lot.
☐ 5. Always remember people's names.
☐ 6. Be a good listener.
☐ 7. Encourage others to talk about themselves.
☐ 8. Compliment other people, even if you don't mean it.
☐ 9. Talk about subjects that interest others.
☐ 10. Call people every day to let them know you are thinking about them.
☐ 11. Show genuine enthusiasm for other people's ideas.
☐ 12. Show your sense of humor to others.
☐ 13. Give people advice frequently.
☐ 14. Be respectful of other people.
☐ 15. Be positive in your ideas and beliefs.
☐ 16. Talk about yourself and your accomplishments.
☐ 17. Complain about everything that bothers you.
☐ 18. Touch the other person frequently.

Answer Key Numbers 1, 4, 5, 6, 7, 9 (come from the book How to Win Friends and Influence People, by Dale Carnegie.) Numbers 11, 12, 14, 15 (come from The Encouragement Book, by Don Dinkmeyer and Lewis E. Losoncy.)

Follow Up What are the three most important ways to make friends? You can use your own ideas.

1. _____
2. _____
3. _____

UNIT TWELVE 53

UNIT 13
Sounds Like a Great Experience...

Let's Start

CONVERSATIONS

ON TAPE — Listen to the conversations <u>two times</u>.
First listen without looking at the book.
Then listen as you read.

1 Talking about places

Have you ever been to Thailand?   Yes, I have. I went there in 1988 with a friend.
What did you think of it?   Oh, I loved it! The countryside is so beautiful.

2 Talking about activities

Have you ever gone hiking in the mountains?   Yes, I have. I hiked in the Sierra Mountains last summer.
Really? What was it like?   It was really fun. It's a great way to relax and enjoy nature.

3 Talking about entertainment

Have you ever been to the theater?   Yes, I have. I saw **Cats** last month.
How was it?   It was wonderful! The music was great.

4 Talking about food

Have you ever tried Korean food?   Yes, I have.
What do you think of it?   It's delicious!

54   UNIT THIRTEEN

Pair Practice

Work in pairs. Make new conversations about your partner's experiences. Use some of the information below.

PARTNER A

1 Have you ever been to _____?
(place)

What did you think of it?
(What was it like?)

PARTNER B

- Yes, I have.
- No, I haven't.

- I loved it.
- I enjoyed it.
- I didn't like it very much.
- I hated it.

2 Have you ever gone _____?
(activities)

What did you think of it?   It was (really)
(How was it?)

- Yes, I have.
- No, I haven't.

- great.
- entertaining.
- fun.
- exciting.
- interesting.
- a little boring.

3 Have you ever been to _____?
(entertainment)

How was it?   It was (really)
(What did you think of it?)

- Yes, I have.
- No, I haven't.

- great.
- entertaining.
- fun.
- exciting.
- interesting.
- a little boring.

4 Have you ever tried _____?
(food)

How was it?   It was
(What did you think of it?)

- Yes, I have.
- No, I haven't.

- delicious.
- wonderful.
- really good.
- okay.
- not very good.
- awful.

---

places
Australia?
Disneyland?
the mountains?
London?
a tropical country?

activities
sailing?
windsurfing?
horseback riding?
swimming in the ocean?
camping?

entertainment
a sumo wrestling match?
a Kevin Costner movie?
a rock concert?
a Country & Western music club?
a Japanese Noh drama?

food
an American cheeseburger?
a German frankfurter?
a Mexican taco?
Japanese sushi?
an Italian pizza?

Social World

A Great Experience

ON TAPE

Listen to these people talking about their experiences.
Put the number of the conversation next to the correct picture.

RIO DE JANEIRO

LONDON

SINGAPORE

MEXICO CITY

SEATTLE

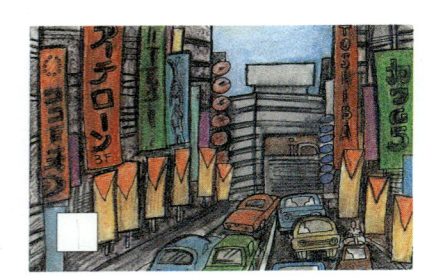

TOKYO

Listen again. What did they think of each place?
Circle (++) if they really liked something, (+) if they liked it, or (-) if they didn't like it.

1
crowds	++	+	−
food	++	+	−
shopping	++	+	−

2
job	++	+	−
weather	++	+	−
people	++	+	−

3
entertainment	++	+	−
buildings (architecture)	++	+	−
restaurants	++	+	−

56   UNIT THIRTEEN

Skill Builders

Sequences

ON TAPE

Listen to each speaker talking about experiences in the past.
How many things do they talk about?
Finish the sentences with the correct number.

1. The speaker lived in ___2___ cities.
2. The speaker had _____ jobs.
3. The speaker traveled to _____ places.
4. The speaker lived in _____ cities.
5. The speaker learned _____ languages.

Listen to each speaker talking about experiences in the past. Then put the events in the correct order by writing 1, 2 or 3 next to each word or phrase.

6. _____ San Francisco
   _____ Chicago
   _____ Boston

7. _____ Florida
   _____ New York
   _____ England

8. _____ California
   _____ Thailand
   _____ Cambodia

9. _____ waiter
   _____ clerk
   _____ cook

10. _____ rock-singer
    _____ accountant
    _____ student

11. _____ had children
    _____ worked
    _____ got married

12. _____ got married
    _____ traveled
    _____ bought a house

13. _____ Fred
    _____ Mike
    _____ Joe

14. _____ Melissa
    _____ Cathy
    _____ Tracy

15. _____ finished school
    _____ worked
    _____ had 10 grandchildren

UNIT THIRTEEN 57

Personal World

A Memorable Place

FOCUS

Do you enjoy travelling? _____
How many countries have you visited? _____
What is one place that is very memorable to you? _____
Why is it so memorable?
_____
Was it something you saw? Something you did? Someone you met?

First Listening...

Listen to the conversations. What places were very memorable for each person? Complete each sentence.

1. Marcia says _____ is a memorable place.
2. Anna says _____ is a memorable place.
3. Nicholas says _____ is a memorable place.
4. Marco says _____ is a memorable place.

Second Listening

Listen again.
What did each person like about the place? Write down one or two words (or phrases).

1. Marcia liked it because: _____
2. Anna liked it because: _____
3. Nicholas liked it because: _____
4. Marco liked it because: _____

A Valuable Experience

FOCUS

What is one experience that was very valuable or important for you?
_____
When did you have this experience? _____

Compare your answers with a partner.

First Listening...

Listen to the conversations.
What valuable experience is each person talking about? Complete each sentence.

1. Tamara's valuable experience was taking _____
2. Ben's valuable experience was visiting _____
3. Yangsu's valuable experience was going to _____

Second Listening...

Listen again. Why was this experience valuable? Complete each sentence.

1. It was the first time that Tamara _____.
2. It was the first time that Ben _____.
3. It was the first time that Yangsu _____.

a. flew in an airplane
b. was able to be independent
c. met a famous person
d. learned about another culture
e. felt the power of nature
f. saw poor people
g. made a friend from another country

58 UNIT THIRTEEN

Conversation Strategies

13: CHECK FOR UNDERSTANDING

Check if your partner understands your meaning.

EXAMPLES (ON TAPE)

- A: How did you feel when you saw Niagara Falls?
  B: I felt really emotional . . . *do you know what I mean?*

- A: What was it like in Bali?
  B: It was so vibrant . . . *do you know what I'm trying to say?*

14: REPHRASE IT

Check your partner's meaning, especially when your partner uses new vocabulary words.

EXAMPLES (ON TAPE)

- A: How did you feel when you saw the Grand Canyon?
  B: I felt really insignificant . . . do you know what I mean?
  A: *I think so. Do you mean small?*

- A: What was it like to see the Pyramids?
  B: It was, I don't know, awesome . . . do you know what I'm trying to say?
  A: *Not exactly. Do you mean wonderful?*

Make short conversations.

Now practice these strategies in new conversations like this:

- A: What was New York like?
  B: It was very hectic . . . do you know what I mean?
  A: I think so. Do you mean busy?
  B: Yes, busy and fast-paced.

1. A: (Mexico City) B: (overwhelming)
   A: (big?)   B: (yes, big and crowded)

2. A: (the temples in Kyoto) B: (elegant)
   A: (beautiful?)   B: (yes, beautiful and graceful)

3. A: (New Zealand) B: (pristine)
   A: (clean?)   B: (no, natural and untouched)

UNIT THIRTEEN   59

UNIT 14

Let's Talk About Travel

Interview

Work with a partner. Write your answers. Then ask your partner. Write down your partner's answers.

Remember to use the Conversation Strategies on page 59.

	COLUMN 1 (YOU)	COLUMN 2 (YOUR PARTNER)
1. Which foreign countries have you visited?	_____	_____
2. What are your impressions?	_____	_____
3. Which foriegn countries would you like to visit?	_____	_____
4. Which cities have you visited in your country?	_____	_____
5. What is a very memorable place for you? Why?	_____	_____
6. Do you think travel is an important part of your growth? How?	_____	_____

Quiz

The First!

Work with a partner. Partner A reads 1, 3, 5, 7, 9, 11. Partner B finds the answers. Partner B reads 2, 4, 6, 8, 10, 12. Partner A finds the answers. Check your answers at the bottom of the quiz.

FIRST EXPERIENCES

1. The first person to cross the Atlantic Ocean alone in an airplane
2. The first rock and roll song
3. The first modern Olympic Games
4. The first telephone
5. The first person to walk on the moon
6. The first blue jeans
7. The first sandwich
8. The first computer
9. The first test tube baby
10. The first human to orbit the earth
11. The first talking motion picture
12. The first Nobel Peace Prize

WHO? WHEN?

a. Alexander G. Bell, the United States, 1876
b. "Baby Louise," England, 1978
c. Bill Haley, *Rock Around the Clock,* 1957
d. Charles Babbage, England, 1822
e. Charles Lindbergh, 1927
f. Earl of Sandwich, England, 1760
g. Greece, 1896
h. Henri Dunant/Switzerland and Frederick Passy/France, 1901
i. Levi Strauss, San Francisco, 1860's
j. Neil Armstrong, 1969
k. *The Lights of New York,* USA, 1928
l. Yuri Gagarin, USSR, 1961

Answer Key

1-e, 2-c, 3-g, 4-a, 5-j, 6-i, 7-f, 8-d, 9-b, 10-l, 11-k, 12-h

On Your Own

Which of these "firsts" has made the greatest impact on your life?

Activity: Sightseeing

Traveling is an excellent way to learn about the world, its people, and its cultures. If some tourists wanted to come to your country to learn about it, what do you think they should do or see? Make a travel plan for a tourist to your country. Here is an example travel plan for some tourists to the United States.

Travel Plan for the United States

NATURAL PLACES	DEVELOPED PLACES	UNUSUAL PLACES
1. the Grand Canyon	Disneyland	Greenwich Village
2. Niagara Falls	New York Stock Exchange	a farm in Iowa
3. the Florida Everglades	Las Vegas	Native American reservation

Three local foods they should try: hot dogs, burritos, Cajun Chicken
Two things they should buy as souvenirs: a cowboy hat, a bottle of California wine
Two activities they should try: go to a rodeo, see a holiday parade

Steps Work with a partner.
1. Complete the travel plan below with things for a tourist to see or do in your country.
2. Give reasons for your choices.
3. Present your list to the class.

Travel Plan for _____

NATURAL PLACES	DEVELOPED PLACES	UNUSUAL PLACES
1. _____	_____	_____
2. _____	_____	_____
3. _____	_____	_____

Three local foods they should try: _____
Two things they should buy as souvenirs: _____
Two activities they should try: _____

Follow Up

Work in a group of four.
Ask your partners these questions:

Do you think it's important for people to travel to other countries?
What can people do to learn about a country before they go there?
What does a tourist need to know about a country to be safe there?

UNIT 15 It's Important to Us.

Let's Start

CONVERSATIONS

First look at the map. Then listen as you look at the map. Find the places on the map.

1 What did you do last weekend?

That sounds like fun. Which park?

Oh, we had a picnic in the park.

The one on Grant Street.

2 What did you do after work last night?

Angelo's? Where's that?

I went to Angelo's Bar to watch the football game.

It's next to the video store on Scott Street.

62 □ UNIT FIFTEEN

3 Did you do anything on Sunday?

Yes, I went swimming.

Oh? Where do you swim?

There's a public pool near my house.

4 What's new with you?

I'm working at a café.

Oh, really? Where is it?

It's across from the new hotel.

5 What have you been doing lately?

I've been working out a lot at the sports club.

Really? Which club do you go to?

It's between the supermarket and the bank on Vincent Street.

6 What shall we do tonight?

Let's rent a movie from the new video store.

New store? Where is it?

It's on the corner of Scott and Green.

Pair Practice

**Work in pairs.
Make new conversations like the ones above.**

1 A: What did you do on Saturday?
   New department store? Where is it?

B: I went shopping at the new department store. It's on . . .

2 A: last weekend?
   _____?

B: went to the new Chinese restaurant (next to)

3 A: after work last Friday?
   _____?

B: went to a dance club with some friends (near)

4 A: on Sunday morning?
   _____?

B: had brunch at the Gatehouse (on the corner of)

5 A: these days?
   _____?

B: taking tennis lessons at the high school (across from)

6 A: tonight?
   _____?

B: working at the movie theater (between)

Social World

Around the City

Listen to these people talking about places around the city. Draw an arrow from each picture to the correct place on the map.

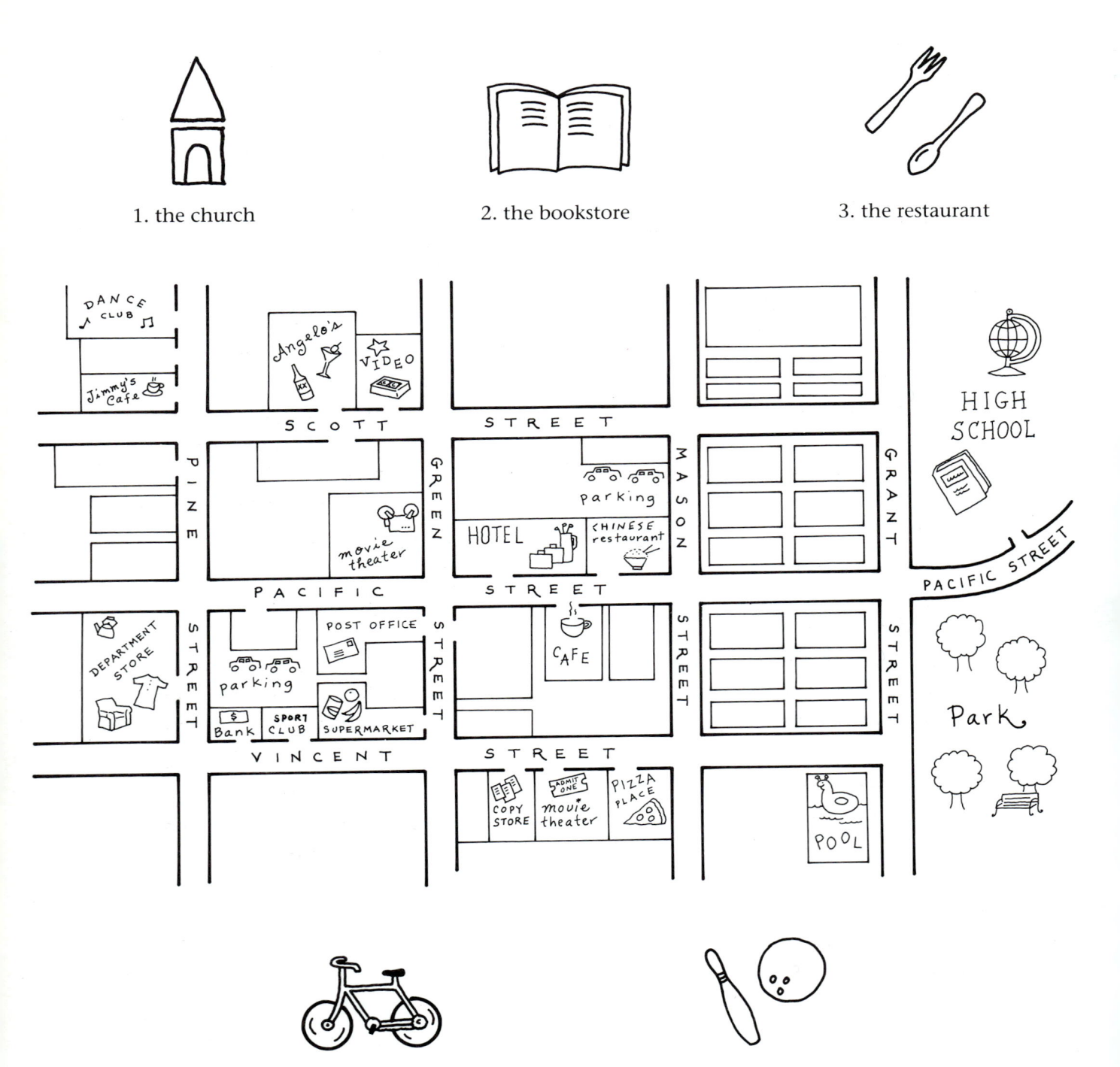

1. the church
2. the bookstore
3. the restaurant

4. the bike shop
5. the bowling alley

UNIT FIFTEEN

Skill Builders: Body Idioms

Listen. The conversation will help you understand the idiom. Circle the correct meaning.

1. **It's on the tip of my tongue.**
   a. I don't know.
   b. I know it but I can't say it.
   c. That's a hard question.

2. **Give me a hand.**
   a. Help me.
   b. Call me.
   c. Give me something.

3. **We don't see eye to eye.**
   a. We don't like each other.
   b. We don't know each other.
   c. We don't agree.

4. **Let's play it by ear.**
   a. Let's make a plan now.
   b. Let's decide later when the time is right.
   c. Let's do it quickly.

5. **Put our heads together.**
   a. Fight about this.
   b. Think of something together.
   c. Sit down together. Change our positions.

6. **It cost an arm and a leg.**
   a. It was very cheap.
   b. It was very reasonable.
   c. It was very expensive.

7. **You're pulling my leg.**
   a. You're fooling me.
   b. You're telling the truth.
   c. You're trying to hurt me.

8. **Learn them by heart.**
   a. Learn to love them.
   b. Translate them.
   c. Memorize them.

9. **Put my finger on it.**
   a. Say the exact reason.
   b. Touch it.
   c. Tell a lie.

10. **Stand on my own two feet.**
    a. Go jogging.
    b. Be independent.
    c. Work hard.

11. **I'm all ears.**
    a. I'm embarrassed by what you are saying.
    b. I'm critical of your news.
    c. I'm ready to listen.

12. **Keep an eye on her.**
    a. Try to find a problem.
    b. Watch over her.
    c. Make her feel ashamed.

13. **Getting in my hair.**
    a. Bothering me.
    b. Brushing my hair.
    c. Hiding from me.

14. **Get it off my chest.**
    a. Take some new responsibility.
    b. Talk about a personal problem.
    c. Move something away.

15. **Keep my head above water.**
    a. Manage in a difficult situation.
    b. Become the leader.
    c. Do as little as possible.

Personal World

Are You Typical?

FOCUS

Read these sentences. Which of them is true for your culture?
Put a check (✔) next to one sentence in each pair.

○ It's good for mothers to stay home with their children.
○ It's good for children to become independent from their parents.
○ It's good for fathers to set the rules of the home.
○ It's good for children to say their opinions about the rules of the home..

○ It's good for people to keep their national traditions.
○ It's good for people to become more modern and international.
○ It's good to be different from other people.
○ It's good to be like other people.

First Listening...
ON TAPE

Listen to these people talking about themselves.
In what way are they <u>typical</u>? Choose one letter (a-e) for each person.

1. Ken _____

a. I watch a lot of television
b. I don't watch television
c. I often play sports
d. I waste a lot of things
e. I work hard

2. Anne _____

a. I'm friendly and outgoing
b. I'm careful with strangers
c. I think everyone has values just like me
d. I don't know much about other countries
e. I know other people have different values

What Is Culture?

FOCUS

Write down one thing that is specific to your culture
(that is, something you find <u>only in your culture</u> and not in any other culture).

_____

Check your idea with a classmate.

First Listening...
ON TAPE

According to each speaker, what is culture?
Match each speaker with his or her definition.

1. Wendy _____   2. Marla _____   3. Henry _____

DEFINITIONS

a. the traditions of a group of people
b. the traditions, the language, and the values
c. the most important ideas and values
d. knowledge about their history
e. the ways that people say and do things
f. the habits and customs of a group of people
g. what the people do most often

66 UNIT FIFTEEN

Conversation Strategies

15: TAKE TIME TO THINK

Take time to think while you are preparing what to say.

EXAMPLES (ON TAPE)

- Who is a typical American?
  Let's see . . . that's a difficult question. . .

- What is a typical American like?
  I don't know exactly . . . let me think . . .

16: CHANGE THE QUESTION

Do this when you want to hear the other person's opinion.

EXAMPLES (ON TAPE)

- What is culture?
  That's a hard question. What do you think?

- What is culture?
  Hmm, I don't know right now. What do you think?

Make short conversations.

Now practice these strategies in new conversations like these:

- A: Is money important in your culture?
  B: Let's see . . . that's a difficult question. I guess it is.

- A: Why is culture important?
  B: Hmm, I don't know right now. What do you think?
  A: Let me think. It might be because people need to follow a pattern.

1. A: What is an important holiday in your country?
   B: _____
   A: _____

2. A: What is an important tradition in your country?
   B: _____
   A: _____

3. A: What is an important belief in your country?
   B: _____
   A: _____

4. Write your own:
   A: _____
   B: _____
   A: _____

UNIT FIFTEEN

UNIT 16

Let's Talk About Culture

Interview

Work with a partner. Write your answers. Then ask your partner. Write down your partner's answers.

Remember to use the Conversation Strategies on page 67.

	COLUMN 1 (YOU)	COLUMN 2 (YOUR PARTNER)
1. What is a typical _____? (examples: student, Japanese, teenager)	_____	_____
2. Are you a typical _____? If no, why not?	_____	_____
3. What parts of your culture are interesting to you? Why? (examples: sports, food, music, behavior, holidays . . .)	_____	_____
4. What parts of your culture are not interesting to you? Why not?	_____	_____

Quiz

Our National Culture

Work with a partner. What best represents your culture? Fill in each line. Then compare your answers with another group. How many of your answers match?

1. a type of music _____
2. a sport _____
3. a place _____
4. an item of clothing _____
5. a food _____
6. a household item _____
7. a hobby or pastime _____
8. a person (from the past or present) _____
9. a festival or holiday _____
10. a writer _____
11. a proverb or saying _____
12. a belief (for example, "people should respect their elders") _____

Activity

Culture Test

In his book, *Cultural Literacy*, E. D. Hirsch, Jr. says that Americans are losing their cultural heritage because children are not learning the important facts of culture.

Work with a partner.

Step 1: Here are some of the items on the Cultural Literacy Test for <u>American</u> culture. How many of these items do you know? Match each question with the correct answer.

AMERICAN CULTURAL LITERACY TEST

1. What is the White House?
2. Where are the Great Lakes?
3. What **food** do Americans traditionally eat on Thanksgiving?
4. What is "This Land is Your Land"?
5. What does this **proverb** mean: "Don't count your chickens before they hatch"?
6. What **holiday** do Americans celebrate on the fourth of July?
7. What is "Jack and the Beanstalk"?
8. What war was fought in the United States between 1861 and 1865?
9. What is Cupid?
10. Where did the words "I have a dream" come from?

Answer Key

1-b, 2-f, 3-i, 4-j, 5-g, 6-d, 7-h, 8-a, 9-e, 10-c.

ANSWERS

a. The **Civil War**
b. The **place** where the President of the United States lives and works
c. These are from a **speech** given by the Rev. Martin Luther King, Jr. in the 1960s. The speech described his dream—to see peace and equality.
d. Independence Day
e. The god of love in Roman **mythology.** When he shot his arrows into people's hearts, they fell in love.
f. In the north-central **part of the** U.S. along the Candian border
g. Don't assume you'll get the things you want before you actually have them.
h. A **fairy tale**
i. Turkey
j. A **folk song** written by Woody Guthrie.

Step 2:

Write a cultural literacy test for your native culture. Include at least one question on:
1. music or songs
2. holidays or festivals
3. language (including idioms and proverbs)
4. government
5. food
6. literature (including mythology, religion, and philosophy)
7. beliefs (including mythology, religion, and philosophy)
8. history of the country
9. geography
10. important people

Step 3:

Exchange tests with another pair. How many questions can you answer?

Follow Up

Work in a group of four. Ask your partners these questions:

Do you think that there are some facts that everyone in your culture should know?

Why or why not?

UNIT 17 What Are You Planning to D[o]

Let's Start

CONVERSATIONS

Listen to the conversations <u>two times</u>.
First listen without looking at the book. Then listen as you read.

1

What are you doing this weekend?
Oh, that sounds like fun.
I'm going to run in a 10K race.

I'm going skiing at Mt. Shasta.
How about you? **What are you doing** this weekend?
Good luck!

2

What are you going to do tonight?
Oh, that doesn't sound very interesting.

I don't know yet. **I might** go to a movie if I'm not too tired.
Thanks. You too.

I think I'll stay home and study.
Yeah, I know. And you?
What are you planning to do?

Well, have fun.

Pair Practice

Work in pairs.
Make new conversations like the ones on the left.

1 What _____ Sunday afternoon?

I _____ wash my car.

I'm _____ to Oshima Beach. How about you?

2 (Friday night?)

(think I'll go dancing with some friends)

(might stay at home and watch a movie on TV)

3 (this weekend?)

(I probably visit my relatives)

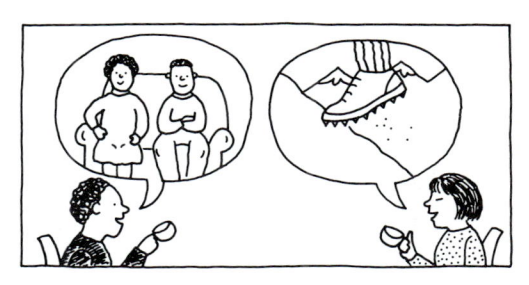

(going hiking on Mt. Takao)

4 (next summer?)

(think I'll learn to play tennis)

(planning to study English in America)

5 (after you finish school?)

(going to get a job)

- (on your next holiday?)
- (next Saturday night?)

_____
YOUR CHOICE
_____
YOUR CHOICE

UNIT SEVENTEEN   71

Social World | **Future Plans**

ON TAPE

Read the events. Then listen to these people talking about their future plans. Write the events on the calendar.

1 go to a party ● watch a tennis match on TV ● read ● work on a paper for school
work in the bookstore ● go to the beach ● play soccer

Mike's Calendar

	SATURDAY	SUNDAY
Afternoon		
Evening		

Paul's Calendar

	SATURDAY	SUNDAY
Afternoon		
Evening		

2 get married ● go to law school ● graduate ● travel
have children ● join a law firm ● save money

Mark's Future Plans

After finishing school	In a few years

UNIT SEVENTEEN

Skill Builders

In Your Future

ON TAPE

In English we can use several forms to show future events. We can choose forms based on whether the events are planned or unplanned, certain or uncertain, and probable or not probable.

Future -- Planned or Unplanned?

Planned -- already decided and fixed
I'm going to play tennis this weekend.
I'm playing tennis with Dave on Saturday.

Unplanned -- not yet decided or fixed
I might play tennis this weekend.
I may play tennis.

Listen to the conversations. Are the activities planned or unplanned? Circle the correct word.

1. Planned   (Not Planned)
2. Planned   Not Planend
3. Planned   Not Planned
4. Planned   Not Planned
5. Planned   Not Planned

Future -- Certain or Uncertain?

Certain -- the speaker is very sure that the event will happen.
I will be in class at 9:15 tomorrow.

Uncertain -- the speaker is not really sure that the event will happen.
I think I'll be here next summer.

Listen to the conversations. Is the speaker certain or uncertain? Circle the correct word.

6. Certain   Uncertain
7. Certain   Uncertain
8. Certain   Uncertain
9. Certain   Uncertain
10. Certain   Uncertain

Future -- Probable or Not Probable?

Probable -- the speaker thinks the event is likely, but can't know for sure.
Jamie will probably be at the party.
The Bears will probably win the game.

Not Probable -- the speaker thinks the event is unlikely, but may happen
I don't think that Jane will be there.
The traffic probably won't be so bad.

Listen to the conversations. Is the event probable or not probable? Circle the correct word.

11. Probable   Not Probable
12. Probable   Not Probable
13. Probable   Not Probable
14. Probable   Not Probable
15. Probable   Not Probable

UNIT SEVENTEEN

Personal World

Advances in the Future

FOCUS

An <u>advance</u> is something new (an invention, a discovery, an idea) that helps people live better lives.
Look at this list of possible advances in the future. Which ones do you think are possible in your lifetime?. Put a check (✔) next to each one.

- ☐ New foods will be developed to feed more people.
- ☐ All nuclear weapons will be destroyed.
- ☐ The world's population will be controlled.
- ☐ A married couple will be able to choose what kind of baby they want.

- ☐ All unpleasant jobs will be done by robots.
- ☐ People won't need eyeglasses anymore.
- ☐ People will begin living in space stations.
- ☐ Doctors will find a cure for all serious diseases, such as cancer and AIDS.

Check your ideas with a classmate.

🎧 First Listening...
ON TAPE

Listen to the conversations. What advances does each person hope for in his or her lifetime? Choose a, b, or c to complete each sentence.

1.
Mark hopes for advances in
_____.

a. population control
b. medicine
c. energy

2.
Jack hopes for advances in
_____.

a. transportation
b. robots
c. clean air

3.
Ruth hopes for advances in
_____.

a. world peace
b. medicine
c. education

4.
Wendy hopes for advances in
_____.

a. country size
b. world peace
c. fighting techniques

Advice to Our Children

FOCUS

What kinds of advice do you think parents should give their children?
(for example: advice about friends, education . . .)

🎧 First Listening...
ON TAPE

Listen to these people talking about important advice for their children's future.
What advice would they give?

1. Mark: _____
2. Jack: _____
3. Ruth: _____
4. Wendy: _____

74 ☐ UNIT SEVENTEEN

Conversation Strategies

17: RESTATE THE IDEA

When you are trying to make a difficult idea clearer, say your idea again in other words.

ON TAPE — EXAMPLES

- I would tell my children to be positive.
  I mean, to be hopeful about the future.

- I want my children to think big.
  What I mean is, to believe they can do anything.

18: SHOW THAT YOU UNDERSTAND

When you understand a difficult idea, tell your partner.

ON TAPE — EXAMPLES

- Children should be hopeful about the future.
  I know what you mean.

- I think it's important to think big.
  I see what you mean.

- To succeed, people must believe they can do anything.
  I understand what you're trying to say.

Make short conversations.

Now practice these strategies in new conversations like these:

- A: What advice would you give your children?
  B: I would tell them to be positive.
  A: I see what you mean.

1. A: What advice would you give your children?
   B: (hopeful, optimistic)
   A: I know what you mean.

2. A: What advice would you give your children?
   B: (trust themselves, believe in their ability)
   A: I understand _____.

3. A: What advice would you give your children?
   B: (learn one thing, do one thing very well)
   A: I see _____.

4. A: What advances do you hope for in the future?
   B: (medical advances, cure for diseases)
   A: I know _____.

5. A: What advances do you hope for in the future?
   B: (world peace, end to war)
   A: I understand _____.

UNIT SEVENTEEN

UNIT 18

Let's Talk About the Future

Interview

Work with a partner. Write your answers. Then ask your partner. Write down your partner's answers.

Remember to use the Conversation Strategies on page 75.

	COLUMN 1 (YOU)	COLUMN 2 (YOUR PARTNER)
1. What are two of the world's most serious problems today?	_____	_____
2. Do you think there will be any advances to help fight these problems in your lifetime?	_____	_____
3. What kind of advances?	_____	_____
4. What advances do you hope for in your lifetime? (new inventions? new ideas?)	_____	_____
5. What will you do personally to help make them happen?	_____	_____
6. What advice would you give to your children for their future?	_____	_____
7. What plans do you have for your future? (education? job? family? lifestyle?)	_____	_____

Quiz

Advances in Our Past

Work with a partner. Here is a list of some important advances in human history. First choose the five advances that you think are the most important. Then compare your choices with another pair. What are your reasons for your choices?

1. _____   2. _____   3. _____   4. _____   5. _____

1903 The Wright Brothers fly the first practical airplane. (United States)
1837 Louis Daguerre invents photography. (France)
1045 Printing is invented. (China)
1796 Edward Jenner introduces vaccination against smallpox. (England)
1946 The first all-electronic computer is invented. (United States)
1957 Sputnik I, the first satellite, is launched into space. (Russia)
1905 Albert Einstein formulates the theory of relativity [$E=mc^2$]. (Switzerland)

c. 105 The process for making paper is developed. (China)
c. 900-750 B.C. Democracy is introduced as a form of government. (Greece)
before 2,000 B.C. The wheel is invented. (Mesopotamia)
c. 650 B.C. Humans learn to make objects from iron. (China)
c. 3100 B.C. The first known writing system is developed. (Mesopotamia)
c. 8000 B.C. Humans begin to farm and settle in villages. (Africa, Asia)
1543 Copernicus declares that the Earth revolves around the Sun. (Poland)
1925 John Baird invents television. (England)

Activity: Fortune Cookie Game

Work with a partner.

Steps
1. Copy these sentences on small strips of paper.
   (Or make a copy of this page and cut out the sentences.)
2. Fold the "fortunes." Place them in a container.
3. Choose one. . . . Does it fit you?

- A mysterious meeting will bring you good news.
- Remember that all mistakes are lessons to be learned.
- The world will soon recognize your greatness.
- You have a great future as an English speaker.
- Good news will come to you from far away.
- You will inherit a large sum of money.
- You will step on the soil of many countries.
- Sing and rejoice, fortune is smiling on you.
- You will win success in whatever you adopt.
- Your future is as boundless as the lofty heaven.
- You are heading in the right direction.
- You will attract cultured and artistic people to your home.
- You will be traveling and coming into a fortune.
- When winter comes, heaven will rain success on you.
- Find release from your cares – have a good time.
- You will have many friends when you need them.
- Good health will be yours for a long time.
- You should be able to undertake and complete anything.
- Your dearest wish will come true.
- Keep your feet on the ground even though friends flatter you.
- You find beauty in ordinary things. Do not lose this ability.
- A cheerful letter or message is on its way to you.

Follow Up

Work in a group of four. Ask your partners these questions:

What does your fortune mean?
What predictions can you make for your classmates?

UNIT EIGHTEEN 77

Tape Script

This is the tape script for the Social World, Skill Builders, and Personal World sections. The narrator's script is contained in the textbook exercises.

Conversation and Conversation Strategy sections are also recorded on tape; the tape script for these sections is on the corresponding exercise pages.

UNIT 1 — *Glad to meet you.*

Social World (page 4)
Student Identification Card Application Form
A: Hello.
B: Hi. I need a student ID card.
A: Sure. What's your name?
B: Alan Worth.
A: Could you spell "Worth?"
B: W O R T H.
A: OK. And what's your address?
B: 3149 South First Street.
A: Could you repeat that, please?
B: Sure. 3149 South First Street. Berkeley, California 94107.
A: OK. And your phone number?
B: Area code 510 —
A: 510 —
B: 945-0109.
A: Did you say 945-0901?
B: No, it's 945-0109.
A: OK. Thank you. That's all. No, wait — What's your Social Security number?
B: Social Security number — it's, um, 778 - 21- 3469
A: 778 - 21 - 3469.
B: Right.
A: OK. Please come back on Friday. Your ID card will be ready then.

Movie Night Video Rentals Membership Application
A: Hello, welcome to Movie Night Video. Can I help you?
B: Yes, I'd like to apply for a membership card.
A: OK. Um, what's your name?
B: It's Rieko Otani.
A: Re—? Um, How do you spell that?
B: R I E K O.
A: R I E K O.
B: And my last name is Otani. O T A N I.
A: O T A N I. Your first name is Rieko and your family name is Otani. Is that right?
B: Yes, that's right.
A: And your address?
B: My address is 120 Elm Street—
A: 120 Elm Street —
B: Mm-hmm. Apartment 4.
A Apartment 4.
B: Dallas, Texas.
A: Dallas, Texas.
B: 70402.
A: 70402. OK, and your phone number, please.
B: Area code 714-454-3859.
A: OK, great. Let's see — We need your driver's license number.
B: Driver's License? Um, here it is — A178462.
A: A178462. OK. That's it. We need a deposit of $25, and then I can issue this card for you.

Skill Builders (page 5)
1. A: Hi. Are you in this class?
   B: Yes, I am. My name's Carol Tanaka.
2. A: Hi, I'm Andre Thompson.
   B: Glad to meet you, Andre.
3. A: Your name, please?
   B: My name? Anna Hinson.
4. A: Hello, I'm Sammy Martinez.
   B: Sorry, what was your last name again?
   A: Martinez.
5. A: My name's Sue Wong.
   B: I'm sorry. Could you spell that, please?
   A: Yes. That's W O N G.
6. A: What's your address?
   B: My address is 201 First Street.
7. A: And your address, please?
   B: I live at 50 Hall Street.
8. A: And your address?
   B: My address? Oh, umm, 1600 Penn Avenue, Apartment C.
9. A: And my address is 1770 Whitehall, Room 102.
   B: Sorry, could you repeat that?
   A: Oh, sure. 1770 Whitehall, Room 102.
10. A: City?
    B: Honolulu, Hawaii 99144.
    A: 99144?
    B: Right.
11. A: What's your phone number?
    B: It's 883-2222.
    A: 2222. Thanks.
12. A: Hello? I'd like the number for Barry Smith, please.
    B: Barry Smith? The number is 445-8901.
13. A: Hello. Could I have the number for June Wilson on California Street?
    B: One moment, please. Yes, that number is 244-6771.
    A: Thanks.
14. A: What city, please?
    B: Los Angeles. I'd like the number for Kyle Woods on Porter Street.

A: One moment. The number is area code 213-662-0905.
B: Thank you.
15. A: What city, please?
B: Boston. I need the number for Susan Snyder. I think she's on Westvale Avenue.
A: One moment, I'll check. Is that S N Y D E R?
B: Yes, um-hm.
A: OK. Here's your number: 617-328-5642.
B: Thanks.

Personal World (page 6)

1.
A: Your name is Mickey, right?
B: Yes. My first name is Mickey. My family name is Harper.
A: How did you get the name Mickey?
B: I was named after Mickey Mantle, the American baseball player.
A: Well, Mickey is an interesting name.
B: Thanks.

2.
A: Your first name is Kate, is that right?
B: Well, actually, my first name is Katherine. My full name is Katherine Rose Lang. My nickname is Kate.
A: Were you named after somebody?
B: Yes, uh-huh. Katherine Rose is my grandmother's name, and I was named after her.
A: It's a beautiful name.
B: Thank you.

3.
A: Your name is Sam, is that right?
B: Yes, my full name is Samuel Edwards, but everyone calls me Sam.
A: Were you named after your father?
B: No. I was named after a famous writer, Samuel Clemens. He was a famous American writer.
A: Sure, I know him.
B: My mother likes his books, so she named me after him.
A: Do you like the name Sam?
B: Yeah, sure.

UNIT 3 *What's Your Schedule?*

Social World (page 12)

1. Sue's Schedule
A: Sue, can I meet you sometime today?
B: Sure, Ted.
A: What's your schedule like today?
B: Let's see. I have classes from 9 o'clock until 11:30, and then I'm going to meet Sam for lunch at 12:00. And I have to work in the library from 2 until 6. Do you want to meet at 6?
A: OK, that sounds good. Let's meet at the library at 6.

2. David's Schedule
A: David, do you want to play tennis next weekend?
B: Yeah, that sounds great.
A: What's your schedule like?
B: Well, on Saturday morning, I'm going to my karate lesson, and on Saturday afternoon I'm going to a wedding.
A: How about Sunday afternoon?
B: Sorry, I can't. I'm going to the movies with Kathy. But I'm free on Sunday morning.
A: OK, I'll get a court for 9 o'clock.

Skill Builders (page 13)

1. A: What time does the class begin?
B: I think it's at 1:15.
2. A: When does the presentation start?
B: It starts at 2:30.
3. A: My class ends at 12:20.
B: OK, I'll see you then.
4. A: When are you free?
B: I'm free at 4.
5. A: What time is the meeting?
B: It's at 9:15.
6. A: When are you leaving?
B: I'm flying to New York at 8:40 p.m.
7. A: What time can you pick me up?
B: I'll pick you up at 6:30 a.m.
8. A: Where are you going?
B: I'm meeting James at 11.
9. A: What time do you leave for work?
B: I leave at 7 in the morning.
10. A: Are you free this evening?
B: No, I'm working until 10.
11. A: Do you want to play tennis this week?
B: Sure. How about on Thursday?
12. A: Are you free this weekend?
B: Well, I'm free Sunday.
13. A: When are you leaving?
B: On Monday.
14. A: When can we talk about the sales report?
B: Hmm. How about on Friday, the 17th?
15. A: Can we meet soon?
B: How about Wednesday, the 23rd.
A: OK.
16. A: Can we meet sometime this week?
B: Sure. Tuesday, the 7th is a good day for me.
A: Tuesday, the 7th. Yes, that's OK.
17. A: When are you going on vacation?
B: My vacation begins on June 25th.
18. A: When's your birthday?
B: My birthday? It's December 12th.
19. A: What's the last day of the semester?
B: I think it's May 13th.
20. A: When do you start your new job?
B: Oh, my new job. On Monday, August 14th.

Personal World (page 14)
I Can't Live Without It

1.
A: What item do you use every day?
B: What item do I use every day? Um, maybe my computer.
A: Your computer?
B: Yes, I work on my computer every day. I write a lot of letters and papers for school.

2.
A: What household item is very important for you?
B: What item is very important for me? Hmm. Let me think. Maybe it's my coffee maker.
A: Your coffee maker?
B: Yes. I love to drink coffee in the morning, so every day when I wake up, I go to the kitchen and make coffee, so my coffee maker is rather important.

3.
A: What item or thing is very important for you?
B: Very important? Hmm. Probably it's my VCR — my video player. I just love to watch videos.

My Favorite Place

1.
A: What room in your house do you use most often?
B: What room? Hmm. I guess it's my kitchen. I spend a lot of time there — reading the newspaper, talking on the telephone, doing my homework, and also just relaxing.

2.
A: What room in your house do you use most often?
B: Which room? Let me think. I guess my bedroom. I have a desk in my bedroom and also a comfortable chair and my stereo set — and of course, my bed. So I spend most of my time reading or listening to music or just thinking — and, of course, sleeping.

3.
A: Which room in your house do you use most often?
B: Which room do I use a lot? Oh, I guess the living room. I spend a lot of time sitting on the couch, just talking to my mother and father and brothers, or watching TV— or eating snacks.

UNIT 5   *Thanks for your help.*

Social World (page 22)
Shopping Spree

1. Well, it's old and it needs a lot of work, but the rooms are large and sunny and it has a very nice garden. If you like to work in the garden, it's perfect for you. Some new paint and a few repairs, and this will be a beautiful place to live.

2. Have you read this one yet? It's wonderful. It's about a family. The story's very sad but the language is so beautiful. In fact, this writer is one of my favorites. I think you'll like it.

3. It's really very simple to use. You just have to dial the number, like on a regular telephone, then put your letter into the slot and you can send a copy of it anywhere in the world. Everybody needs one, and this model is not very expensive.

4. Now this is a lovely one. It's 100% cotton — very soft and completely washable. You can wear it with pants or skirts. I think these colors will look wonderful on you.

5. I think this is just the one for you. It's completely automatic so you can't make a mistake, and it has a zoom lens so you can take good close-up pictures. I have this exact model, and I use it a lot. It takes great pictures.

The Right Price

1. A: Excuse me. I'm looking for a Japanese-English dictionary.
   B: Well we have two fine ones over here.
   A: Hmm. How much are they?
   B: The student dictionary is $13.50, and the translator's dictionary costs $19.95.
   A: OK, thank you. I'll look at both of them.

2. A: I'm looking for a used car — something about $6,000.
   B: Well, we have two models that you might like. This one's an '89 Cyprus. It looks great, and we're asking $6,500 for it. We also have a '91 Mantra. It's a beautiful car in great condition, and it's $7,500.
   A: Hmm. That's a big difference.

3. A: Can I help you?
   B: Yes, I'm looking for some things for my apartment. Can you tell me the price of this desk and this lamp?
   A: Certainly. The desk is $179, and the lamp is on sale for $62.50.
   B: I see. And how about this bookshelf?
   A: That's on sale too, for $89.
   B: OK, thank you. I'd like to think about it.

4. A: Excuse me. How much is this sweater?
   B: Let's see. It's $36.
   A: OK, I'll take it. And these jeans too, please.
   B: Fine. The jeans are $29. Now can I show you anything else? Maybe a jacket?
   A: Well, all right. How much is this one?
   B: That's $58. Why don't you try it on?

Skill Builders (page 22)

1. There are 21 new students.
2. We need 115 books.
3. There are 14 men in the class.
4. 1,001 people will fit in this room.
5. She's 27 years old.
6. 3,020 people live in this town.
7. There are 1,150 people who work for this company.
8. This car was driven 55,500 miles.
9. That city has a population of 129,000.
10. I think there are about 6,000 students at this university.
11. It's $35.59.
12. That one's only $5.50.
13. That comes to $124.77.
14. It's on sale for $880.
15. I'm selling it for $2,600.
16. A: The total is $7,600.
    B: How much is that in Japanese yen?
    A: That's almost ¥1,000,000.

17. A: That costs $409.
    B: How much is that in Korean wan?
    A: That's about ₩313,000.

18. A: The total is $7,600.
    B: How much is that in Canadian dollars?
    A: It's about CAN$9000.

19. A: This one costs $9,950 (99-50).
    B: What is that in German marks?
    A: Let's see — that's about DM15,600.

20. A: The asking price is 4 million.
    B: 4 million dollars! What is that in Taiwanese dollars?
    A: That's over NT98 million.

Personal World (page 23 & 24)
Shopping
1.
A: What was the last thing that you bought?
B: The last thing I bought? What do you mean?
A: I mean a major purchase — over $100.
B: The last thing I bought over $100? I guess it was this suit. I bought this suit last week. It's an Italian suit made by Armani. Do you know that designer?
A: Yes, mm-hm. It's nice. I like that light brown color.

2.
A: What was the last thing that you bought?
B: I'm not sure what you mean. Do you mean the last big thing?
A: Yeah. What was the last big thing you bought?
B: Hmm. I guess my car. I bought a used car last month.
A: Oh, a used car?
B: Yes. It's a 1990 Toyota Celica. It's kind of a small car, very comfortable — a sort of dark red. I really like it.

3.
A: What was the last thing that you bought?
B: I think it was my CD player. I bought a new CD player about a month ago.
A: A CD player?
B: Right. It's a Sony. It's a new model, very small, very compact, very good speakers — easy to use. Here, let's listen to something. (plays some music)
A: Nice.

Clothes
1.
A: What clothes do you wear most often?
B: What clothes? Probably jeans and a sweater, a light sweatshirt and running shoes That's what I tend to wear most of the time. I especially like to wear light blue — blue is my favorite color.

2.
A: What clothes do you wear most often?
B: Wear most often? Well, I'm at work for eight or more hours every day, so I guess a suit. I always wear a dark suit to work. I love dark, deep colors. Most of my suits are dark grey and dark blue.

3.
A: What clothes do you wear most often?
B: Wear most often? I usually wear shorts and a jacket, especially this jacket I'm wearing now — this bright green color. I really like this color. A lot of my clothes are green.

UNIT 7 *What is she like?*

Social World (page 30)
Describing People
A: Do you know all of these people?
B: Well, they're my friends from college. I know most of them.
A: Wow, there are so many people here! I'll never remember their names.
B: Don't worry, I'll help you. Oh, there's James Parker.
A: James Parker?
B: Yes, he's the one with short blond hair and a mustache, about average height. Can you see him?
A: Where?
B: Over there. He's wearing a light brown jacket with dark green pants and a colorful tie.
A: Oh, yes, I see him.
_____
B: And there's his wife, Maria Chacon.
A: Maria Chacon.
B: Yeah, there she is. Do you see the tall woman with long dark hair?
A: Tall with long dark hair?
B: Yes. She's about 25, and she's wearing a short black dress with a pink jacket and a big gold necklace.
A: Uh-huh, I see her. So, that's Maria.
_____
A: And which one is Laura Davis? You're always talking about her.
B: Hmm, let's see. Where is Laura? She's not very tall. She's got short brown hair and a big smile —
A: Is she the woman wearing the orange sweater with a black and orange skirt, and the high heeled shoes?
B: Yeah, that's her.
_____
A: And Laura is married to — ?
B: She's married to Ken Matsumura. Let's see, where is he? Ken has dark hair and glasses and is about six feet tall. There he is. He's wearing a grey jacket, a white shirt —
A: Oh, yeah. I see him.
_____
B: Look, Alice is here.
A: Who?
B: Alice Choy. See the woman with curly black hair and the pretty eyes? She's wearing a dark blue dress with a belt and big earrings.
A: Oh, yes, so that's Alice Choy.
B: So can you remember their names?
A: Oh, gee, I don't think so — um, Alice, Ken, James, Maria, Laura —

Skill Builders (page 31)

1. Do you know John? (# = short pause)
First sentence: (slow) Do#you know John?
Second Sentence: (fast) <u>Do you</u> know John?

2. Did you meet Paula?
First sentence: (fast) <u>Did you</u> meet Paula?
Second sentence: (slow) Did#you meet Paula?

3. No, who is she?
First sentence: (slow) No, who is#she?
Second sentence: (fast) No, who <u>is she?</u>

4. You're going to like John.
First sentence: (slow) You're going#to like John.
Second sentence: (fast) You're <u>going to</u> like John.

5. He's wearing a nice shirt.
First sentence: (fast) He's wearing a <u>nice shirt</u>.
Second sentence: (slow) He's wearing a nice#shirt.

6. I want you to meet Alice.
First sentence: (fast) I <u>want you</u> to meet Alice.
Second sentence: (slow) I want#you to meet Alice.

7. Did you see Maria?
First sentence: (slow) Did#you see Maria?
Second sentence: (fast) <u>Did you</u> see Maria?

8. Do you see the tall slim woman?
First sentence: (slow) Do#you see the tall slim woman?
Second sentence: (fast) <u>Do you</u> see the tall slim woman?

9. Yes, I'd like to meet her.
First sentence: (fast) Yes, I'd <u>like to</u> meet her.
Second sentence: (slow) Yes, I'd like#to meet her.

10. Could you introduce us?
First sentence: (slow) Could#you introduce us?
Second sentence: (fast) <u>Could you</u> introduce us?

11. Have you seen them?
12. What do they look like?
13. I don't know.
14. Yes, I met her.
15. She asked me to dance.
16. She's one of my friends.
17. He has blond hair and glasses.
18. You're always talking about him.
19. He's wearing a T-shirt and a tie!
20. Let's go talk to them.

Personal World (page 32)
Personalities
1.
A: How do people describe your personality?
B: Gee, I don't know — I guess "friendly." Most people think that I'm friendly.
A: Why do they think so?
B: Well, I'm usually smiling and cheerful.

2.
A: How do people describe your personality?
B: Hmm, I don't know. Some of my friends tell me that I'm serious — that I look serious.
A: Oh, really? Why do they say that?
B: They say it's because I look like I'm always thinking about something very important and serious.

3.
A: How do people describe your personality?
B: Hmm. How do people describe me? I guess they'd say I'm honest.
A: Why honest?
B: Well, I always say what I think or feel. Sometimes other people don't like it — but they know I'm honest.

Friends
1.
A: Tell me about your best friend.
B: My best friend is Lauren. She's, what, thoughtful and deep, but also funny — has a great sense of humor. A nice person to be around — she makes me feel alive.
A: It sounds like she's fun to be with.
B: Oh, yeah! She really is.

2.
A: Can you tell me about your best friend.
B: I guess my best friend is Erik. He's, well, he has so many sides to him. Sometimes he's very funny and lovable — laughing and happy — and other times he gets very serious and can get very angry. So he's got these different sides to him.
A: So would you say he's hard to understand?
B: Hmm, yeah — right.

3.
A: Could you tell me about your best friend?
B: My best friend is Anatoly. He's not like other people. He's kind of weird, but he's really artistic. He can draw and paint and write music. That's what makes him interesting to me — he can do so many different things.
A: So would you say he's unique?
B: Oh, yes. Absolutely.

UNIT 9 *I'm Getting Better.*

Social World (page 40)
1.
A: (shivering) Brrrr...
B: What's the matter?
A: It's really cold in here. Would you mind closing the windows?
B: Sure, no problem.

2.
A: So what do you want to do this weekend?
B: I don't know. Something different.
A: I know. Let's rent a boat and go sailing.
B: Hey, that sounds great!

3.
A: Hey, Bruce?
B: Yeah?

A: I was wondering — is it OK if I borrow your car? I only need it for about an hour.
B: Hmm, I guess so. Sure. The keys are on the table.
4.
A: What's this?
B: Just a little gift for you.
A: Wow, that's really nice of you. Oh, it's beautiful! Thank you so much!
B: You're welcome. I knew you'd like it.
5.
A: Janet, your sister just told me it was your birthday last week. I'm really sorry I forgot.
B: Oh, well. That's OK.
A: Happy late birthday anyway. I hope it was nice.
6.
A: Jane, wait a second. I want to ask you something.
B: What is it?
A: Would you like to go to a concert with me on Saturday?
B: Oh, I'm sorry. I can't on Saturday.
7.
A: John, wait a second — I want to ask you something.
B: What is it?
A: Would you like to go to a concert with me on Saturday?
B: Oh, that'd be great. I'd love to go.

Skill Builders (page 41)

1. I'm sorry I missed class yesterday. I wasn't feeling well.
2. Would you mind answering the phone? My hands are wet.
3. Could I borrow your calculator for a minute?
4. Thanks a lot for helping me with my homework.
5. Are you coming over for dinner tonight?
6. What should we do tonight?
7. Well, I'd better go. Talk to you later.
8. Oh, no, I forgot all about our meeting. I'm sorry.
9. Carlos, this is Rita. Rita, this is my friend Carlos.
10. It's going to be a great party. I'll bring the pizza.
11. Well, I have to get going. See you tomorrow.
12. I have an idea. Let's go downtown for dinner tonight.
13. I have to go to the bank. Would you mind waiting for me?
14. Julie, I'd like you to meet Tom. Tom, this is Julie.
15. There were so many people in the line at the bank. I'm sorry I kept you waiting so long.
16. I'll be ready at 8:00. What time will you be here?
17. Hey, James. Is it OK if I borrow one of your CDs?
18. If you're free tonight, would you like to have dinner with me?
19. I don't really want to drive. Let's take the train instead.
20. I really like the watch you gave me. Thanks a lot.

Personal World (page 42)

A Second Language
1.
A: What's your second language?
B: My second language? French, I guess. I studied it in high school and college.
A: Was it easy or difficult to learn?
B: It was difficult — especially pronunciation. There are a lot of sounds that are difficult for me. I still have an American accent, but I'm getting better.
2.
A: What's your second language?
B: Japanese. I've been speaking Japanese since I was a child.
A: Was it easy or difficult to learn?
B: Oh, I'd say it was pretty easy for me. My grandmother's Japanese, and she lived with us, so she always spoke to me in Japanese.
A: So it was easy to learn Japanese?
B: Conversation was easy, but I had a very hard time with writing, remembering the Kanji — you know the writing system. It took so much time to learn to write.
3.
A: How long have you been studying English?
B: A long time — about ten years. I studied in high school and university. And after university, I went to Australia for one year.
A: Is English easy or difficult for you to learn?
B: For me it's really difficult. I still have a lot of problems with grammar, especially verbs. English has so many verb tenses for different situations. It's very confusing.

A Good Language Learner
1.
A: What do you think makes a good language learner?
B: Hmm. I'm not sure. I think a good language learner is someone who has a good memory, someone who can remember new vocabulary, since vocabulary is so important when you learn a second language.
A: Yeah, I think so too.
2.
A: What do you think makes a good language learner?
B: Well, I guess a good language learner is someone who practices a lot outside of class — someone who will try to speak the language every day. I think it's like sports — the more you practice, the better you get.
A: Yes, I know what you mean.
3.
A: What do you think makes a good language learner?
B: I think to be a good language learner you have to be really interested in the language and the culture.
If you're interested then you'll probably pay more attention and you'll probably practice more. People who have a strong reason to learn probably learn better.
A: Yeah, that's for sure.

UNIT 11   *What do you do?*

Social World (page 48)
1.
A: Wow, it's really cold today.
B: I know. And I forgot to wear my coat. I'm freezing!
A: Do you work around here?
B: Yeah, I work in the Sears building.
A: Really? So do I. What floor?
B: The 20th.
A: Oh. I'm on the 34th.

2.
A: Wow, this is really a hard class. What do you think of it?
B: I think it's confusing sometimes. Dr. Smith doesn't explain things very well.
A: Are you a biology major?
B: Yeah, I'll be finished next year. How about you?
A: No, I'm an English major.

3.
A: How's it going?
B: Pretty good.
A: You a friend of Dan's?
B: Yeah, we play soccer together. How about you? You play soccer?
A: Nah, I'm into biking.

4.
A: Excuse me, don't you work in the international department?
B: Yes, I do.
A: So do I. I handle accounts for North and South America.
B: Oh, really? I do the East Asia accounts.
A: I thought so. By the way, my name's Vivian Marconi.
B: Nice to meet you. I'm Pete Nash.

Skill Builders (page 49)

1. A: This is a great party, isn't it?
   B: It sure is.
2. A: Is this your coat?
   B: Um-hmm, it is.
3. A: You a friend of Dave's?
   B: Yeah, we work together.
4. A: Do you play soccer?
   B: Yeah, I play on the weekends sometimes.
5. A: Can I get you something to drink?
   B: Hunh-unh, thanks.
6. A: Beautiful day, isn't it?
   B: It's wonderful!
7. A: Want a drink?
   B: Sure, I'd love one.
8. A: Hey, how you doing?
   B: Hi, what's up?
9. A: Are you from around here?
   B: No, I'm from San Francisco.
10. A: I'm a receptionist. You?
    B: I'm a waiter.
11. A: You play tennis?
    B: No, I don't.
12. A: Nice day, isn't it?
    B: Yeah, it really is.
13. A: Want a drink?
    B: No, thanks. I'm fine.
14. A: You work here?
    B: Yeah, I do. Do you?
15. A: You a student here?
    B: Yeah, I am. You?
16. A: I'm from Atlanta. You?
    B: I'm from Seattle.
17. A: You know Masa?
    B: Yes, we work together.
18. A: How you doing?
    B: Good. And you?
19. A: Great party, isn't it?
    B: Yeah, it sure is.
20. A: You a chef too?
    B: No, I'm a cashier.

Personal World (page 50)
Making Friends

1.
A: Is it easy for you to make friends?
B: No, it's not, frankly. I have a hard time making friends.
A: Hmm.
B: Yes, usually I need someone to introduce me to new people.
A: Can you give me an example?
B: Well, for example, last week I was at a party at my friend Mike's house, and I had to wait for Mike to introduce me to one of his friends — and then I was able to start talking to him.

2.
A: Is it easy for you to make friends?
B: Uh, well, yes, sort of.
A: What do you mean?
B: Well, I can go up to people and be very friendly, or act very friendly.
A: Can you give me an example?
B: For instance, at school, during the breaks I can talk to other students easily and laugh and make jokes.

3.
A: Is it easy for you to make friends?
B: Oh, yes, absolutely, I make new friends all the time.
A: How do you do it?
B: Well, when I meet new people, I try to show interest. I find out what they're interested in and I start talking about that.
A: Like what? Can you give me an example?
B: Well, I was in the supermarket this morning, and this woman was buying flowers, and I just started talking to her about flowers and gardening and things. It's really easy for me.

Meeting Friends

1.
A: Where did you meet most of your friends?
B: Mostly at school. Almost all of my friends are school friends. I've known them since grade school or high school.
A: Oh, really? Like who?
B: Well, Laura — I've known her since we were in seventh grade. And Molly, I've known her since the first grade.

2.
A: Where did you meet most of your friends?
B: Work, I guess. I meet lots of people at work, and some of them I get to know socially.
A: What do you mean? Can you give me an example?
B: Well, if I meet someone at work that I like, we go out and do things together outside the office — like eat dinner in a restaurant or watch football games on TV, stuff like that.

UNIT 13   *Sounds like a great experience!*

Social World (page 56)
A Great Experience

1.
A: Have you ever been to Japan?
B: Yes, I was there on a business trip last year. But I was only able to visit Tokyo.
A: So what was it like?
B: The crowds were terrible! But even so, it's a very clean place.
A: How about the food? What did you think of it?
B: I loved it. The fish, especially, was really delicious. I think I ate fish every day.
A: How was the shopping?
B: Good. You can buy anything you want in Tokyo.

2.
A: Have you ever lived outside of California?
B: Yes, I lived in Seattle for two years.
A: Oh, really? Why did you go there?
B: Well, I left college. I wanted a change, so I went to Seattle to work on a fishing boat.
A: To work on a fishing boat?
B: Yes, the job was great! Very interesting work and very good pay, too. And I worked hard. It was good for my health.
A: Yeah? Well, how was the weather in Seattle? I hear it can be really bad.
B: Oh, yeah. The weather was terrible. It was always rainy and cool. I didn't like it very much.
A: What about the people in Seattle? What were they like?
B: Really nice. People there are very relaxed and friendly. It was easy to make friends.

3.
A: Have you ever lived in a big city?
B: No, I never wanted to. How about you?
A: I have. I lived in London for three years.
B: Really? What did you think of it?
A: I liked it. In a big city there's always something to do, so I went to concerts and museums and the theater a lot. London has the best entertainment.
B: London is pretty famous for its architecture, isn't it? What did you think of it?
A: I thought it was really great. I spent a lot of time just walking through the city and looking at the buildings.
B: How were the restaurants?
A: They were OK. I managed to find some good ones in my neighborhood. Yeah, London was a good place to live.

Skill Builders (page 57)

1. We don't move around much. I was born and grew up in Florida, and then after I got married, we settled in Atlanta. We've been here ever since.

2. After college, I got a job in a bank. Then I quit and started my own restaurant business, but I had some problems so after about five years I got another job at an oil company.

3. Oh, I love to travel. My first big trip was to Mexico. That was beautiful. Then a few years later I went to Egypt, and last year I went to Bali in Indonesia. I'd love to go back there!

4. Last year I was living in Houston because I was going to school there, and before that I lived in New York. Actually I was born in New York and lived there for the first three years of my life — and then last month I moved back to New York again.

5. Traveling is a lot more fun if you can speak the language. I first learned French in high school. Then in college I took up Russian — that was really hard. And a few years later I started learning Japanese. That really helped me a lot when I traveled to Japan.

6. I was born in Chicago. Then my family moved to the West Coast, so I grew up in San Francisco. And then I went to college in Boston.

7. After I got married, we moved to Florida. Before that I lived in New York — but I was actually born in England.

8. We escaped from Cambodia in 1988. Then we lived at a camp in Thailand for two years — and finally we immigrated to California in 1990.

9. My first job was as a waiter — I did that for about three years. And then I went to a different restaurant and got a job as a cook, which I did for four or five years. After that I worked as a clerk in an insurance office.

10. I'm an accountant now, but when I was a teenager I tried to be a rock star. But I wasn't a very good singer, so I went to college to get a degree, and here I am in this office.

11. I got married right after high school. It seemed like the right thing to do at the time. I worked in a supermarket for a while, and then I quit and had three children.

12. I didn't want to settle down right away, so before I got married I traveled a lot. I even lived in Singapore for a while. After we were married for several years, we bought this house.

13. My husband's name is Joe, but he's not my first husband. My first husband, Fred, died in the war. I was single for a long time before I met my second husband, Mike. It was a bad marriage, and so we got divorced.

14. Yeah, I always had a lot of girlfriends in high school. I was really in love with Cathy, but that didn't last too long. And then I met Melissa. Oh, I forgot about Tracy — I went out with Tracy before I met Cathy.

15. Well, I always liked school, but when I was 14 I had to quit and go to work. I worked for 53 years, had a family, even had 10 grandchildren. This year I finally went back and finished college, at the age of 68!

Personal World (page 58)
A Memorable Place

1.
A: Tell me about one place that you think is really memorable.
B: Alaska. It's unlike any place I've ever been — so natural, so open, so beautiful. It's really hard to describe. For me it was like going to the moon. Everything was so grand. I just felt insignificant. Do you know what I'm trying to say?
A: Umm, not exactly.
B: The land and the mountains and the glaciers are so big that I really felt small. For the first time, I understood how small human beings are. It was really a memorable experience for me.

2.
A: What place was really memorable for you?
B: Paris. It's the most wonderful place, because Paris is both old and new. It's full of history and also modern architecture and ideas. Everywhere you look you find modern art, fashion, culture. It's just so vibrant. Do you know what I mean?
A: I think so. Do you mean busy?
B: No, not just busy, I mean exciting and alive.

3.
A: Of all the places you've visited, which one is really memorable?
B: I'd say Hawaii. It's gorgeous! I mean it has beaches, mountains, rain forests, canyons, even volcanoes. It's really the perfect place for an outdoor person. And the lifestyle is so different. Do you know what I mean?
A: I'm not sure. Can you give me an example?
B: Well, people move at a slower pace. Whenever I'm there, I feel so relaxed.

4.
A: Tell me about one place that was really memorable to you.
B: I'd say the Great Wall in China. It's awesome.
A: Do you mean really big?
B: Yeah. It's huge, much bigger than I imagined it — and so strong and well-built. It's the most incredible thing I've ever seen.

A Valuable Experience

1.
A: Can you tell me about one valuable experience for you?
B: Sure. Once I took a boat trip down the Colorado River, in the Grand Canyon. That was really amazing! I think it was a great experience because it was the first time I really felt the power of nature.

2.
A: Can you tell me about one valuable experience for you?
B: Hmm, a valuable experience. Well, I especially remember going to a big city for the first time when I was about fifteen. I think that was really the first time that I had ever seen poor people, homeless— people who just stood on the street and asked you for money. And I guess I finally realized that not everyone has a home and enough money. I learned that I was actually very comfortable.

3.
A: Can you tell me about one valuable experience for you?
B: Oh, yes. I always think that the most valuable experience in my life was when I went to Mexico. I was 23. This was a great experience for me. You see, my parents didn't want me to go. They thought I was too young. They said I should stay at home and work and find a husband. But I went to Mexico anyway. It was the first time I was able to be independent.

UNIT 15   *It's important to us.*

Social World (page 64)

1.
A: What time does the wedding start, honey?
B: At 11. By the way, do you know where the church is?
A: Uh-huh. It's on Grant Street across from the high school.
B: Oh, that's right.

2.
A: What did you do last night?
B: Oh, I spent a few hours at the bookstore.
A: A few <u>hours</u>? Wow! Which bookstore was it?
B: City Books. It's near the post office on Pacific Street.

3.
A: Did you do anything on Saturday night?
B: Yeah, I went out for a hamburger with my roommate.
A: Really? Where did you go?
B: It's a little place on Pine Street between the dance club and Jimmy's Café.

4.
A: Are you working now?
B: Yeah, I have a job at a bike shop.
A: That sounds interesting. Where is it?
B: It's across from Angelo's Bar on Scott Street.

5.
A: What do you want to do tonight?
B: Let's go bowling!
A: Hey that's a good idea. Where can we go?
B: There's a bowling alley on the corner of Pine and Scott. Let's try that one.

Skill Builders (page 65)

1. It's on the tip of my tongue.
A: What's your history professor's name?
B: It's umm — oh, wait... Pro, Pora — it's on the tip of my tongue. Ah, why can't I remember it!?

2. Give me a hand.
A: I have a lot of things to do today, but I don't have much time. Can you give me a hand?
B: Sure. What do you want me to do?

3. We don't see eye to eye.
A: Do you like George?
B: Sure I do, but we don't always see eye to eye. His opinions are really different from mine.

4. Let's play it by ear.
A: Do you want to go to the park on Saturday, or would you rather see a movie?
B: I don't know yet. Let's play it by ear and see what the weather will be like, and then we can decide.

5. **Put our heads together.**
A: What should I get Mom for her birthday? I don't know what she'd like.
B: Don't worry, I'll help you. I'm sure if we put our heads together, we'll find something.

6. **It cost an arm and a leg.**
A: What did you think of that new Italian restaurant?
B: The food was good, but it cost an arm and a leg. I spent almost $100!

7. **You're pulling my leg.**
A: Hey, did you know that I met the president when I was in Washington?
B: That's not possible! You're pulling my leg.

8. **Learn them by heart.**
A: These idioms are so strange. I don't really know how to use them.
B: You should just learn them by heart. Just keep repeating them. Then you'll remember them.

9. **Put my finger on it.**
A: Why don't you like this apartment?
B: I don't know exactly. I can't put my finger on it, but something's not right.

10. **Stand on my own two feet.**
A: If you need money, you should ask your parents for help.
B: No, I want to stand on my own two feet. I'll do it by myself.

11. **I'm all ears.**
A: Let me tell you about my new class.
B: Go ahead. I'd love to hear about it — I'm all ears.

12. **Keep an eye on her.**
A: I need to run to the store for a minute, but my baby's still sleeping. Can you keep an eye on her until I get back?
B: Sure, don't worry. I'll watch her.

13. **Getting in my hair.**
A: What's wrong?
B: Oh, I can't finish my work. The kids keep getting in my hair. They won't leave me alone.

14. **Get it off my chest.**
A: Are you busy?
B: Not at all, why?
A: Well, I have a big problem and I just have to get it off my chest. I need to talk to someone.

15. **Keep my head above water.**
A: How are you doing in your new job?
B: (sighs) Oh, It's really tough for me. I'm working hard, but I've got so much to do — I'm just trying to keep my head above water.

Personal World (page 66)

Are you typical?

1.
A: Do you think you're a typical American?
B: A typical American? I'm probably a typical American in that I'm very wasteful and I think Americans are really wasteful.
A: Can you give me an example of how you're wasteful?
B: Hmm. Well, like garbage. I throw out a lot of garbage and that's probably pretty typical. And gasoline — I drive everywhere and use a lot of gasoline.

2.
A: Do you think you're a typical American?
B: Oh, probably in some ways. I think most Americans are really outgoing and try to be friendly, in general, and I think I'm like that too.

What Is Culture?

1.
A: What is your definition of culture?
B: That's a hard question. Maybe culture is what the people of a place know about their history.

2.
A: What is your definition of culture?
B: You know, I think culture is just what the people in a country do most often in their daily life — like eat hamburgers and watch TV. If that's what they do, that's their culture.

3.
A: What is your definition of culture?
B: Hmm, let me think. I think culture is what people consider to be their most important ideas and values. So for example, if people consider freedom or personal choice to be very important, then that's part of their culture.

UNIT 17 *What are you planning to do?*

Social World (page 72)

1.
A: Hey, Mike! What are you going to do this weekend?
B: Well, I'm going to be pretty busy. On Saturday afternoon I'm playing soccer with some friends. Then on Saturday night I'm going to a party with my girlfriend.
A: And on Sunday?
B: I have to work on a term paper, so I'm going to study in the library for a few hours on Sunday afternoon. How about you? What are you doing this weekend?
A: Oh, I'm working all day at the bookstore on Saturday, and I think I'll just stay home and read on Saturday night.
B: What about Sunday?
A: My roommate and I — we're going to ride our bikes down to Redondo Beach.
B: That's a long way!
A: Yeah, it'll probably take three or four hours.
B: Are you going to study this weekend?

2.
A: Are you graduating this semester, Mark?
B: Yes, I am. Only one more month of school.
A: Well, what are you going to do when you're finished?
B: First, I'm going to move to New York.
A: Really? What for?
B: I'm going to go to law school at New York University. I think I'll like it. Everyone says New York's an exciting city. Well, after I graduate in a few years, I'll get a job, maybe in New York. I'd like to work for a law firm.
A: Do you think you'll ever get married?
B: I do want to get married someday, but not right now. You know, I think that's something you just can't decide.

Skill Builders (page 73)

1. A: What are you doing tonight?
   B: I don't know. I might go to a café after dinner.

2. A: How about you? What are you doing?
   B: I'm going to have dinner with a friend.

3. A: Do you have any plans for the weekend?
   B: Yeah, I'm going camping at Mt. Shasta.

4. A: Hey, are you doing anything tomorrow?
   B: Well, I may drive to the beach if the weather's good.

5. A: Do you want to have lunch together today?
   B: I can't. I'm meeting my boss for lunch at 12:30.

6. A: What are you going to study at the university?
   B: I think I'll major in economics.

7. A: Are you free on Saturday?
   B: Sorry. I'll be working on Saturday.

8. A: I hope you can come to the party tonight.
   B: Sure I can. I'll be there at nine.

9. A: When are you going on vacation?
   B: I think I'll leave on the 22nd.

10. A: When can I call you?
    B: Anytime. I'll be home all day tomorrow.

11. A: Are you still going out with Nancy?
    B: Uh-huh. We'll probably get married this year.

12. A: Hey, what's wrong?
    B: I'm late! I don't think I'll finish this report on time.

13. A: When is Pablo coming back?
    B: He'll probably be back in a few minutes.

14. A: You look terrible!
    B: I _feel_ terrible. I probably won't go to work today.

15. A: Uh-oh. It looks like rain.
    B: Oh, no! I don't think we'll be able to play tennis today.

Personal World (page 74)
Advances in the Future
1.
A: What advances do you hope for in the future?
B: Advances for the future? I'd like to see real advances in medicine — what I mean is, how to cure diseases, like cancer and AIDS, and how to prevent problems like heart attacks.

2.
A: What advances do you hope for in your lifetime?
B: You know, what I hope for — is sensible transportation. I mean, the use of cars and gasoline is way out of control. I really would like to see advances in transportation that would be cleaner — and healthier.

3.
A: What advances do you hope for in your lifetime?
B: What I hope for is advances in education. In my opinion, education is the key to the future. We've got to find ways to be sure that everyone gets an education. That's one advance I hope for.

4.
A: What advances do you hope for in the future?
B: I hope for world peace. There are so many problems in the world — so much fighting in countries, people within countries and between countries. I hope we'll find a way to end the fighting.

Advice to Our Children
1.
A: What advice would you like to give to your children for their future?
B: Advice for their future? I think I'd want to say, "Do one thing well." I mean, choose one thing that you love to do, and really learn to do it well — with your whole mind and heart. Because then they'll always have something special that they can be proud of, something that makes them special.
A: So you would say, "Do one thing well?"
B: Yes, that's my advice.

2.
A: What is the best advice you could give to your children for their future?
B: The best advice, I think, is join with other people — work together. What I mean by that is that you can't achieve anything by yourself, but you can do wonderful things if you join with others. So I would tell them, "Join with other people."

3.
A: What do you think is the best advice you might give to your children for the future?
B: The best advice — I think it's to tell them to think big. What I mean is, we often don't challenge ourselves very much. We think too small, like "I can't do this" or "I can't do that." I want my children to have confidence in themselves, to believe that they can do anything.
A: So you would tell them to think positively?
B: Not only that. I would tell them to think big.

4.
A: What would be the best advice for your children's future?
B: Hmm. I guess I would tell them to be hopeful about the future. I mean, there are a lot of problems in life, everyone has problems — but you have to get through them. And I think if my children are positive and hopeful, they _will_ get through their problems, and they'll have a happier life.
A: So you would say, "Be hopeful."
B: Absolutely.

CONVERSATION STRATEGIES

STRATEGY #1. (page 7)

> **Show interest**

Show interest in your partner's information.
- *Oh, that's an interesting name.*

STRATEGY #2. (page 7)

> **Ask for repetition**

If you don't hear correctly, ask your partner to say it again.
- *I'm sorry, what's your name again?*

STRATEGY #3. (page 15)

> **Repeat the question**

Do this when you need time to think.
- *What's my favorite food?*

STRATEGY #4. (page 15)

> **Think out loud**

Do this to show that you understand the question.
- *Hmm...Maybe...*

STRATEGY #5. (page 25)

> **Check it out**

When your partner's question is not clear, ask for clarification.
- *I'm not sure what you mean.*

STRATEGY #6. (page 25)

> **Confirm it**

Try this to check if your partner understands your meaning.
- *Do you know that movie?*

STRATEGY #7. (page 33)

> **Give a summary**

Express your partner's meaning in your own words.
- *It sounds like...*

STRATEGY #8. (page 33)

> **Ask a summary question**

Ask about your partner's meaning in your own words.
- *Do you mean that...?*

STRATEGY #9. (page 43)

> **Show agreement or disagreement**

Respond to your partner's opinion.
- *I'm not sure about that.*

STRATEGY #10. (page 43)

Show something in common

Show you have the same feeling or experience.
- *I do too. / I don't either.*

STRATEGY #11. (page 51)

Ask for examples

When you want more information, ask for examples.
- *Can you give me an example?*

STRATEGY #12. (page 51)

Offer an example

When your partner wants more information, offer an example.
- *I go to a lot of places. For example, ...*

STRATEGY #13. (page 59)

Check for understanding

Check if your partner understands your meaning.
- *Do you know what I mean?*

STRATEGY #14. (page 59)

Rephrase it

Check your partner's meaning, especially when your partner uses new vocabulary words.
- *Do you mean...?*

STRATEGY #15. (page 67)

Take time to think

Take time to think while you are preparing what to say.
- *Let me think.*

STRATEGY #16. (page 67)

Change the question

Do this when you want to hear the other person's opinion.
- *That's a difficult question. What do you think?*

STRATEGY #17. (page 75)

Restate the idea

When you are trying to make a difficult idea clearer, say your idea again in other words.
- *What I mean is...*

STRATEGY #18. (page 75)

Show that you understand

When you understand a difficult idea, tell your partner.
- *I know what you mean.*